Colourful
Baby Crochet

Colourful
Baby Crochet

35 adorable and easy patterns
for babies and toddlers

Laura Strutt

CICO BOOKS
LONDON NEW YORK

For Ethan Wolf and Elkie Raven
– fiercely and forever.

Published in 2023 by CICO Books
an imprint of Ryland Peters & Small Ltd
20–21 Jockey's Fields, London WC1R 4BW

www.rylandpeters.com

10 9 8 7 6 5 4 3 2 1

A CIP catalogue record for this book is available
from the British Library.

ISBN: 978 1 80065 255 2

Printed in China

Editor: Marie Clayton
Pattern checker: Jemima Bicknell
Designer: Alison Fenton
Photographer: James Gardiner
Stylist: Nel Haynes

In-house editor: Jenny Dye
Art director: Sally Powell
Creative director: Leslie Harrington
Production manager: Gordana Simakovic
Publishing manager: Penny Craig

MIX
Paper | Supporting
responsible forestry
FSC® C008047

Contents

Introduction

Crochet is a craft that brings me so much joy. I love the whole process, from choosing the yarns and selecting the colours to falling into the meditative rhythm of working the stitches. Of course, seeing a finished piece always gives a huge dopamine hit. One of the best parts about designing and crocheting for babies and small children is that the makes are often smaller and quicker to make. Not to mention the fact that they are also super cute.

I really enjoyed crocheting things for my children when they were small babies, and I've always loved to give handmade items to celebrate new arrivals. I wanted this collection of garments, accessories, blankets and toys to be bright and fun – not only to look at but also to make. I love bold colours and my children got so much joy from wearing every shade of the rainbow, usually all at the same time!

The colourful projects in this book are fantastic for using up yarns from your stash, or for taking with you to work on-the-go as they are small and portable. This not only makes it easier to fit some crochet into our busy lives, but also means these projects are ideal for beginners. Working on bite-sized makes boosts your creative confidence, and small-scale designs like the ones in this book are great for trying out different techniques and crochet stitches. These projects use a range of skills including working in the round, lace patterns, amigurumi (a method of creating 3D items such as toys) and more.

Crochet is kindness – first to yourself for taking the time to create something, and then as a second joy when you share your makes with your children or give them as gifts. I hope that you enjoy these projects as much as I enjoyed creating them.

Happy crocheting,
Laura

Size chart

Some of the garments have instructions for different sizes, which have been designed according to the following guide. Check this chart before you decide which size to make. If the child you're making the garment for is in between sizes, make the larger size.

AGE	HEIGHT	CHEST	WEIGHT
3–6 months	68cm (27in)	43cm (17in)	13lbs 4oz (8kg)
6–9 months	74cm (29in)	45cm (18in)	17lbs 10oz (9kg)
9–12 months	80 cm (31in)	47cm (18.5in)	19lbs 13oz (10kg)
12–18 months	86cm (34in)	49cm (19.25in)	22lbs (11kg)
18–24 months	94cm (37in)	51cm (20in)	24lbs 4oz (12.5kg)
24–36 months	96.5cm (38in)	52cm (20.5in)	32lbs (14.5kg)

chapter 1

Clothes & Accessories

Slip-on Booties

Warm booties are a wardrobe staple for tots – this easy-on design is worked in the round with no uncomfortable seams. The use of plush chenille yarn makes them ultra cosy.

SKILL RATING: ●●

YARN AND MATERIALS

James C Brett Flutterby Chunky (100% polyester) chunky (bulky) yarn, approx. 175m (191yd) per 100g (3½oz) ball
  1 ball each of:
  Grey Blue B44 (blue) or
    White BO1 (A)
  Parchment B36 (beige) or
    Pink B34 (B)

HOOK AND EQUIPMENT

5.5mm (US size I/9) hook

Stitch markers (optional)

Yarn needle

FINISHED MEASUREMENTS

Length of sole: 11cm (4¼in)

Width of sole at widest: 7cm (2¾in)

Height to cuff top (when folded): 8.5cm (3¼in)

TENSION (GAUGE)

16 sts x 8 rows measure 10cm (4in) working half treble, using 5.5mm (US size I/9) hook.

ABBREVIATIONS

See page 126.

Booties

SOLE

Using A, ch10.

Round 1: 2htr in 2nd st from hook, 1htr in next 7 ch, 5htr in last ch, rotate work and cont along second side of ch, 1htr in next 7 ch, 2htr in last ch, join with a sl st in first st. *(23 sts)*

Round 2: Ch1 (does not count as a st throughout), [2dc in next st] twice, 1dc in next 4 sts, 1htr in next 3 sts, [2htr in next st] 5 times, 1htr in next 3 sts, 1dc in next 4 sts, [2dc in next st] twice, join with a sl st in top of first st. *(32 sts)*

Round 3: Ch1, [1htr in next st, 2htr in next st] twice, 1htr in next 7 sts, [1htr in next st, 2htr in next st] twice, 2htr in next 2 sts, [1htr in next st, 2htr in next st] twice, 1htr in next 7 sts, [1htr in next st, 2htr in next st] twice, join with a sl st in top of first st. *(42 sts)*

TIPS This design is worked in the round, meaning there will be no seams on the finished bootie for added comfort; using locking stitch markers will help you to keep your place in the pattern.

When working with chenille yarn make a knot in the end of the yarn, this will help prevent the end from fraying.

Make it yours

Make the design brighter by working the upper portion in stripes by alternating yarns A and B on each round.

UPPER SECTION

Round 4: Change to B, ch1, 1dc BLO in each st around, join with a sl st BLO in top of first st.

Round 5: Ch1, 1htr in each st around, join with a sl st in top of first st.

Round 6: Ch1, 1dc in next 11 sts, 1htr in next st, [htr2tog, 1htr in next st] twice, [tr2tog, 1dc in next st] 3 times, tr2tog, [1htr in next st, htr2tog] twice, 1htr in next st, 1dc in next 6 sts, join with a sl st in top of first st. *(34 sts)*

Round 7: Ch1, 1dc in next 13 sts, 1htr in next st, htr2tog, [tr2tog] 4 times, htr2tog, 1htr in next st, 1dc in next 7 sts, join with a sl st in top of first st. *(28 sts)*

Round 8: Ch1, 1dc in next 12 sts, 1htr in next st, [tr2tog] 4 times, 1htr in next st, 1dc in next 6 sts, join with a sl st in top of first st. *(24 sts)*

Round 9: Ch1, 1dc in next 10 sts, 1htr in next st, [tr2tog] 4 times, 1htr in next st, 1dc in next 4 sts, join with a sl st in top of first st. *(20 sts)*

ANKLE CUFF

Round 1: Ch1, 1dc in each st around, join with a sl st in first st.
Fasten off B.

Rounds 2–4: Change to A, ch3 (counts as 1tr), 1tr in each st around, join with a sl st in 3rd of 3-ch.

Round 5: Ch2 (counts as 1htr), 1htr in each st, join with a sl st in 2nd of 2-ch.
Fasten off.

Making up and finishing

Ensure all cut yarn ends have a neat knot and weave in securely (see page 123).

Baby Bonnet

The crochet shell stitch adds a classic style to this baby bonnet, and working in colourful stripes gives it a modern finish. The bonnet features a flat seam at the back to ensure a comfortable fit for baby.

SKILL RATING: ● ●

YARN AND MATERIALS

Debbie Bliss Baby Cashmerino (55% merino wool, 33% acrylic, 12% cashmere) baby (sport) weight yarn, approx. 125m (137yd) per 50g (1¾oz) ball
  1 ball each of:
  Silver 12 (A)
  Mint 3 (B)
  Lilac 10 (C)
  Speedwell 97 (blue) (D)

HOOK AND EQUIPMENT

3.5mm (US size E/4) hook

Yarn needle

SIZES

0–3 mth: **3–6 mth**

FINISHED MEASUREMENTS

0–3 mth: crown to neck 12.5cm (5in), back of head to front 12.5cm (5in), ties 25cm (10in)

3–6 mth: crown to neck 16.5cm (6½in), back of head to front 16.5cm (6½in), ties 25cm (10in)

TENSION (GAUGE)

4 shells x 11 rows measure 10cm (4in) working shell stitch, using 3.5mm (US size E/4) hook.

ABBREVIATIONS

See page 126.

Make it yours

The bonnet is created with a folded and seamed rectangle; you can adapt the size by working a larger or smaller rectangle. The foundation chain needs to be a multiple of six chain stitches plus two to create the stitch pattern.

Bonnet

Using A, ch62:**74**.

Row 1: 1dc in 2nd ch from hook, 1dc in each st to end, turn. *(61:**73** sts)*

Row 2: Ch1 (does not count as a st throughout), 1dc in first st, *miss 2 sts, 5tr in next st, miss 2 sts, 1dc in next st; rep from * to end. *(10:**12** shells)*

Row 3: Change to B, ch3 (counts as 1tr throughout), 2tr in same st, miss 2 sts, 1dc in next st, miss 2 sts, *5tr in next st, miss 2 sts, 1dc in next st, miss 2 sts; rep from * to last st, 3dc in last st, turn.

Row 4: Change to C, ch1, 1dc in first st, *miss 2 sts, 5tr in next st, miss 2 sts, 1dc in next st; rep from * to end, turn.
Row 5: Change to D, ch3, 2tr in same st, miss 2 sts, 1dc in next st, miss 2 sts, *5tr in next st, miss 2 sts, 1dc in next st, miss 2 sts; rep from * to last st, 3dc in last st, turn.
Row 6: Change to B, ch1, 1dc in first st, *miss 2 sts, 5tr in next st, miss 2 sts, 1dc in next st; rep from * to end, turn.
Row 7: Change to C, ch3, 2tr in same st, miss 2 sts, 1dc in next st, miss 2 sts, *5tr in next st, miss 2 sts, 1dc in next st, miss 2 sts; rep from * to last st, 3dc in last st, turn.
Row 8: Change to D, ch1, 1dc in first st, *miss 2 sts, 5tr in next st, miss 2 sts, 1dc in next st; rep from * to end, turn.
Rows 9–14: Rep Rows 3–8.
Row 15: Rep Row 3.

SIZE 3–6M ONLY

Rows 16 and 17: Rep Rows 4 and 5.

BOTH SIZES

Next row: Change to A, ch1, 1dc in first st, *miss 2 sts, 5tr in next st, miss 2 sts, 1dc in next st; rep from * to end, turn.
Next row: Cont in A, ch3, 2tr in same st, miss 2 sts, 1dc in next st, miss 2 sts, *5tr in next st, miss 2 sts, 1dc in next st, miss 2 sts; rep from * to last st, 3dc in last st, do not turn.

TIES

Ch51, 1htr in second ch from hook, 1htr in each ch to end. *(50 sts)*
Sl st in corner of bonnet, cont working down side of bonnet, ch1, 30dc along side of bonnet.
Fasten off.
Rejoin A and rep for second side.
Fasten off.

JOIN BACK SEAM

Rejoin A at one end of foundation row and work 72 sts evenly along length.
With bonnet folded in half and back seam aligned, *insert hook from front to back through first st, draw yarn through then insert hook front to back through corresponding st on other side, draw yarn through, yarn round hook and draw through all three loops on hook; rep from * to end.
Fasten off.

Making up and finishing

Weave in yarn ends neatly, and block neatly to finished measurements (see page 123).

Colourblock Mittens

Mittens are a cold weather staple, ideal for keeping little hands warm when out for a walk or a trip to the park. These mittens feature a smaller thumb-free design for younger babies and a larger style with separate thumb for toddlers.

SKILL RATING: ●

YARN AND MATERIALS

Paintbox Yarns Baby DK (55% nylon 45% acrylic) DK (light worsted) weight yarn, approx. 167m (183yd) per 50g (1¾oz) ball

  1 ball each of:
  Vanilla Cream 706 (A)
  Washed Teal 732 (B)
  Bubblegum Pink 750 (C)
  Pistachio Green 724 (D)

HOOK AND EQUIPMENT

4mm (US size G/6) hook

Stitch markers (optional)

Yarn needle

SIZES

0–3 mth: **3–6 mth:** 9–12 mth

FINISHED MEASUREMENTS

0–3 mth: length from folded cuff to tip 7.5cm (3in), width at centre 5cm (2in)

3–6 mth: length from folded cuff to tip 11.5cm (4½in), width at centre 6.5cm (2½in)

9–12 mth: length from folded cuff to tip 13cm (5¼in), width to base of thumb 7cm (2¾in)

TENSION (GAUGE)

6 sts x 5 rows measure 2.5cm (1in) working double crochet, using 4mm (US size G/6) hook.

ABBREVIATIONS

See page 126.

Mittens size 0–3 mth

RIBBED CUFF

Using A, ch7.

Row 1: 1dc in 2nd ch from hook, 1dc in each ch to end, turn. *(6 sts)*

Rows 2–16: Ch1 (does not count as a st throughout), 1dc BLO in each dc to end, turn.

Fold work in half across width aligning current row with foundation chain. Join with a sl st to make a round (cuff will be closed later).

HAND

Turn work onto side so you are working into row ends, ch1, 1dc in end of each row, join with a sl st in first st. *(16 sts)*

Begin working in rounds.

Round 1: Ch1, 1dc in each st to end, join with a sl st in first st.

Round 2 (inc): Change to B, ch1, 1dc in next 6 sts, 2dc in next st, 1dc in next 7 sts, 2dc in next st, 1dc in last st, join with a sl st in first st. *(18 sts)*

Round 3 (inc): Ch1, 1dc in next 7 sts, 2dc in next st, 1dc in next 8 sts, 2dc in next st, 1dc in last st, join with a sl st in first st. *(20 sts)*

Round 4 (inc): Ch1, 1dc in next 8 sts, 2dc in next st, 1dc in next 9 sts, 2dc in next st, 1dc in last st, join with a sl st in first st. *(22 sts)*

Round 5: Change to C, ch1, 1dc in each st to end, join with a sl st in first st.

Rounds 6 and 7: Ch1, 1dc in each st to end, join with a sl st in first st.

Round 8: Change to D, ch1, 1dc in each st to end, join with a sl st in first st.

Rounds 9 and 10: Ch1, 1dc in each st to end, join with a sl st in first st.

Round 11 (dec): Change to A, ch1, 1dc in next 7 sts, [dc2tog] twice, 1dc in next 6 sts, [dc2tog] twice, 1dc in last st, join with a sl st in first st. *(18 sts)*

Round 12: Ch1, 1dc in each st to end, join with a sl st in first st.

Round 13 (dec): Ch1, 1dc in next 5 sts, [dc2tog] twice, 1dc in next 5 sts, [dc2tog] twice, join with a sl st in first st. *(14 sts)*

Round 14: Ch1, 1dc in each st to end, join with a sl st in first st.

Round 15 (dec): Ch1, [dc2tog] 7 times, join with a sl st in first st. *(7 sts)*

Fasten off, leaving enough yarn to sew top of mitten.

Making up and finishing

Weave in all ends, draw up yarn at the opening at the top of the mitten and sew closed. Block neatly to measurements (see page 123).

Make it yours

For older children, work a long length of chain stitches in your chosen colour and then work a double crochet in each stitch to create a cord. Attach one end to each mitten and thread through the sleeves of a coat to prevent losing a mitten.

NOTE: Be cautious of long strings of cord with very young children because they can pose a choking hazard.

TIPS When working the colour changes, make a small knot at the join of the two yarns and hold the ends against the work. By working over the yarns when you work the next stitches, you will have made a start on securing in the ends for weaving in.

When working the base of the thumb on the largest size, be sure that the stitches are picked up neatly around the section so that the thumb portion has no gaps where it meets the mitten.

Mittens size 3–6 mth

RIBBED CUFF

Using A, ch11.

Row 1: 1dc in 2nd ch from hook, 1dc in each ch to end, turn. *(10 sts)*

Rows 2–20: Ch1 (does not count as a st throughout), 1dc BLO in each dc to end, turn.

Fold work in half across width aligning current row with foundation chain. Join with a sl st to make a round (cuff will be closed later).

HAND

Turn work onto side so you are working into row ends, ch1, 1dc in end of each row, join with a sl st in first st. *(20 sts)*

Begin working in rounds.

Rounds 1 and 2: Ch1, 1dc in each st to end, join with a sl st in first st.

Round 3 (inc): Change to B, ch1, 1dc in next 8 sts, 2dc in next st, 1dc in next 9 sts, 2dc in next st, 1dc in last st, join with a sl st in first st. *(22 sts)*

Round 4 (inc): Ch1, 1dc in next 9 sts, 2dc in next st, 1dc in next 10 sts, 2dc in next st, 1dc in last st, join with a sl st in first st. *(24 sts)*

Round 5 (inc): Ch1, 1dc in next 10 sts, 2dc in next st, 1dc in next 11 sts, 2dc in next st, 1dc in last st, join with a sl st in first st. *(26 sts)*

Round 6: Change to C, ch1, 1dc in each st to end, join with a sl st in first st.

Rounds 7 and 8: Ch1, 1dc in each st to end, join with a sl st in first st.

Round 9: Change to D, ch1, 1dc in each st to end, join with a sl st in first st.

Rounds 10 and 11: Ch1, 1dc in each st to end, join with a sl st in first st.

Round 12 (dec): Change to A, ch1, 1dc in next 9 sts, [dc2tog] twice, 1dc in next 8 sts, [dc2tog] twice, 1dc in last st, join with a sl st in first st. *(22 sts)*

Round 13 (dec): Ch1, 1dc in next 7 sts, [dc2tog] twice, 1dc in next 6 sts, [dc2tog] twice, 1dc in last st, join with a sl st in first st. *(18 sts)*

Rounds 14 and 15: Ch1, 1dc in each st to end, join with a sl st in first st.

Round 16 (dec): Ch1, 1dc in next 5 sts, [dc2tog] twice, 1dc in next 5 sts, [dc2tog] twice, join with a sl st in first st. *(14 sts)*

Round 17: Ch1, 1dc in each st to end, join with a sl st in first st.

Round 18 (dec): Ch1, [dc2tog] 7 times, join with a sl st in first st. *(7 sts)*

Fasten off, leaving enough yarn to sew top of mitten.

Making up and finishing

Weave in all ends, draw up yarn at the opening at the top of the mitten and sew closed. Block neatly to measurements.

Mittens size 9–12 mth

RIBBED CUFF

Using A, ch17.

Row 1: 1dc in 2nd ch from hook, 1dc in each ch to end, turn. *(16 sts)*

Rows 2–22: Ch1 (does not count as a st throughout), 1dc BLO in each dc to end, turn.

Fold work in half across width aligning current row with foundation chain. Join with a sl st to make a round (cuff will be closed later).

HAND

Turn work onto side so you are working in row ends, ch1, 1dc in end of each row, join with a sl st in first st. *(22 sts)*
Begin working in rounds.

Round 1: Ch1, 1dc in each st to end, join with a sl st in first st.

Round 2 (inc): Change to B, ch1, 1dc in next 9 sts, 2dc in next st, 1dc in next 10 sts, 2dc in next st, 1dc in last st, join with a sl st in first st. *(24 sts)*

Round 3 (inc): Ch1, 1dc in next 10 sts, 2dc in next st, 1dc in next 11 sts, 2dc in next st, 1dc in last st, join with a sl st in first st. *(26 sts)*

Round 4 (inc): Ch1, 1dc in next 11 sts, 2dc in next dc, 1dc in next 12 sts, 2dc in next dc, 1dc in last st, join with a sl st in first st. *(28 sts)*

Round 5: Ch1, 1dc in each st to end, join with a sl st in first st.

Round 6: Change to C, ch1, 1dc in each st to end, join with a sl st in first st.

Round 7: Ch1, 1dc in next 11 sts, miss next 5 sts (thumb), ch5, 1dc in next 12 sts, join with a sl st in first st.

Round 8: Ch1, 1dc in next 11 sts, 1dc in each ch (5 sts), 1dc in next 12 sts, join with a sl st in first st. *(28 sts)*

Round 9: Ch1, 1dc in each st to end, join with a sl st in first st.

Round 10: Change to D, ch1, 1dc in each st to end, join with a sl st in first st.

Rounds 11–13: Ch1, 1dc in each st to end, join with a sl st in first st.

Round 14 (dec): Change to A, ch1, 1dc in next 10 sts, [dc2tog] twice, 1dc in next 9 sts, [dc2tog] twice, 1dc in last st, join with a sl st in first st. *(24 sts)*

Round 15: Ch1, 1dc in each st to end, join with a sl st in first st.

Round 16 (dec): Ch1, 1dc in next 9 sts, [dc2tog] twice, 1dc in next 7 sts, [dc2tog] twice, join with a sl st in first st. *(20 sts)*

Round 17: Ch1, 1dc in each st to end, join with a sl st in first st.

Round 18 (dec): Ch1, 1dc in next 7 sts, [dc2tog] twice, 1dc in next 5 sts, [dc2tog] twice, join with a sl st in first st. *(16 sts)*

Round 19 (dec): Ch1, [dc2tog] 8 times, join with a sl st in first st. *(8 sts)*

Fasten off, leaving enough yarn to sew top of mitten.

THUMB

Rejoin A to thumb hole base, 12dc around thumb hole. *(12 sts)*

Round 1: Ch1 (does not count as a st throughout), 1dc in each st to end, join with a sl st in first st.
Rep Round 1 a further 4 times.

Next round: Ch1, 1dc, dc2tog, 5dc, dc2tog, 2dc, join with a sl st in first st. *(10 sts)*

Next round: Ch1, [dc2tog] 5 times, join with a sl st in first st. *(5 sts)*

Fasten off, leaving enough yarn to sew top of thumb.

Making up and finishing

Weave in all ends, draw up yarn at the opening at the top of the mitten and thumb and sew closed. Block neatly to measurements (see page 123).

Bear Beanie

Stay cute and cosy with this adorable bear-ears hat. Worked in a soft and chunky yarn, this beanie hat is quick to make and will help little ones beat the chills on cold days.

SKILL RATING: ●

YARN AND MATERIALS

Deramores Studio Chunky Acrylic (100% acrylic) chunky (bulky) weight yarn, approx. 80m (87yd) per 100g (3½oz) ball

1 ball each of:

Spice 70830 (brown) (A)

Oatmeal 70805 (light brown) (B)

HOOK AND EQUIPMENT

7mm (US size K/10½–L/11) hook

Stitch marker (optional)

Yarn needle

SIZES

0–3 mth: **3–6 mth:** 6–12 mth

FINISHED MEASUREMENTS

0–3 mth: lower edge to crown 12.5cm (5in), width across lower edge 15cm (6in) measured flat

3–6 mth: lower edge to crown 15cm (6in), width across lower edge 18cm (7in) measured flat

6–12 mth: lower edge to crown 16cm (6¼in), width across lower edge 20cm (7¾in) measured flat

TENSION (GAUGE)

11 sts x 8 rows measure 10cm (4in) working half treble, using 7mm (US size K/10½–L/11) hook.

ABBREVIATIONS

See page 126.

TIPS Using stitch markers is a great way to keep track of the start of the round; this will help you to keep the work even.

When creating the ear embellishments, leave longer yarn tails and use these to secure the pieces to the top of the hat.

Make it yours

This hat is worked from the top – the crown – down, so you can adapt the size for a custom fit by increasing or decreasing the numbers of stitches that form the top of the hat and the number of rounds worked.

Beanie

Using A, make a magic ring.
Round 1: Ch1 (does not count as a st throughout), 6htr into ring, join with a sl st in first st. *(6 sts)*
Round 2: Ch1, 2htr in each st around, join with a sl st in first st. *(12 sts)*
Round 3: Ch1, *2htr in next st, 1htr in next st; rep from * around, join with a sl st in first st. *(18 sts)*
Round 4: Ch1, *2htr in next st, 1htr in next 2 sts; rep from * around, join with a sl st in first st. *(24 sts)*
Round 5: Ch1, *2htr in next st, 1htr in next 3 sts; rep from * around, join with a sl st in first st. *(30 sts)*

SIZES 3–6 MTH AND 6–12 MTH ONLY

Round 6: Ch1, *2htr in next st, 1htr in next 4 sts; rep from * around, join with a sl st in first st. *(36 sts)*

SIZE 6–12 MTH ONLY

Round 7: Ch1, *2htr in next st, 1htr in next 5 sts; rep from * around, join with a sl st in first st. *(42 sts)*

ALL SIZES

Next round: Ch1, 1htr in each st around, join with a sl st in first st. *(30:**36**:42 sts)*
Rep last round 5 more times. *(6 rows total)*
Change to B, work last round once more.
Next round: 1dc BLO in each st around, join with a sl st in first st.
Fasten off and weave in ends.

Ears

(make 2)
Using B, make a magic ring.
Round 1: Ch1 (does not count as a st throughout), 6htr into ring, join with a sl st in first st. *(6 sts)*
Row 1 (RS): Ch1, 2htr in each st around, do not join. Fasten off. *(12 sts)*
Row 2: With RS facing, join A to first st, ch1, 1dc in each st to end.
Fasten off, leaving a long tail of yarn to secure to the beanie.

Making up and finishing

Position the ears onto the upper section of the hat, pin in place and ensure both are aligned neatly.
Sew securely into place.
Weave in all ends and block neatly to measurements (see page 123).

Bandana Bib

For teething and weaning the bandana bib is a must-have baby accessory. This simple triangle design is worked in 100 per cent cotton yarn, making it both easy-care for frequent washing and gentle against baby's skin.

SKILL RATING: ●

YARN AND MATERIALS

Lily Sugar 'n Cream Ombre (100% cotton) aran (worsted) yarn, approx. 86m (94yd) per 55g (2oz) ball
  1 ball each of:
  Potpourri Prints 00178 (cream mix) (A)
  Psychedelic 02600 (brights mix) (B)

HOOK AND EQUIPMENT

4.5mm (US size 7) hook

Yarn needle

Wooden button, 2cm (¾in) diameter

FINISHED MEASUREMENTS

Along neckline: 39cm (15¼in)

Down centre line to point: 22cm (8¾in)

TENSION (GAUGE)

14 sts x 8 rows measure 10cm (4in) working half treble, using 4.5mm (US size 7) hook.

ABBREVIATIONS

See page 126.

Bib

Using A, make a magic ring.
Foundation row: Ch1 (does not count as a st), 5dc into ring, turn. *(5 sts)*
Row 1: Ch2 (does not count as a st throughout), 2htr in first stitch, 1htr in next st, 3htr in next st (centre line), 1htr in next st, 2htr in last st, turn. *(9 sts)*
Row 2: Ch2, 2htr in first st, 1htr in next 3 sts, 3htr in next st (centre line), 1htr in next 3 sts, 2htr in last st, turn. *(13 sts)*
Row 3: Ch2, 2htr in first st, 1htr in next 5 sts, 3htr in next st (centre line), 1htr in next 5 sts, 2htr in last st, turn. *(17 sts)*
Row 4: Change to B, ch2, 2htr in first st, 1htr in next 7 sts, 3htr in next st (centre line), 1htr in next 7 sts, 2htr in last st, turn. *(21 sts)*
Row 5: Change to A, ch2, 2htr in first st, 1htr in next 9 sts, 3htr in next st (centre line), 1htr in next 9 sts, 2htr in last st, turn. *(25 sts)*
Row 6: Ch2, 2htr in first st, 1htr in next 11 sts, 3htr in next st (centre line), 1htr in next 11 sts, 2htr in last st, turn. *(29 sts)*
Row 7: Ch2, 2htr in first st, 1htr in next 13 sts, 3htr in next st (centre line), 1htr in next 13 sts, 2htr in last st, turn. *(33 sts)*
Row 8: Change to B, ch2, 2htr in first st, 1htr in next 15 sts, 3htr in next st (centre line), 1htr in next 15 sts, 2htr in last st, turn. *(37 sts)*

Make it yours

Create a second bib and invert the colourways to make use of the remaining yarn and create a set of two co-ordinating bibs.

TIPS This bib is worked backward and forward in rows, turning the work after each row is completed. The increases at the centre create the triangle, bandana shape.

Select a flat button over a raised, shank style button; this will be more comfortable against baby's neck. Be sure to sew the button fastening on securely so that it does not pose a choking hazard.

Row 9: Change to A, ch2, 2htr in first st, 1htr in next 17 sts, 3htr in next st (centre line), 1htr in next 17 sts, 2htr in last st, turn. *(41 sts)*

Row 10: Ch2, 2htr in first st, 1htr in next 19 sts, 3htr in next st (centre line), 1htr in next 19 sts, 2htr in last st, turn. *(45 sts)*

Row 11: Ch2, 2htr in first st, 1htr in next 21 sts, 3htr in next st (centre line), 1htr in next 21 sts, 2htr in last st, turn. *(49 sts)*

Row 12: Change to B, ch2, 2htr in first st, 1htr in next 23 sts, 3htr in next st (centre line), 1htr in next 23 sts, 2htr in last st, turn. *(53 sts)*

Row 13: Change to A, ch2, 2htr in first st, 1htr in next 25 sts, 3htr in next st (centre line), 1htr in next 25 sts, 2htr in last st, turn. *(57 sts)*

Row 14: Ch2, 2htr in first st, 1htr in next 27 sts, 3htr in next st (centre line), 1htr in next 27 sts, 2htr in last st, turn. *(61 sts)*

Row 15: Ch2, 2htr in first st, 1htr in next 29 sts, 3htr in next st (centre line), 1htr in next 29 sts, 2htr in last st, turn. *(65 sts)*

Fasten off A.

BORDER

Change to B, ch2, 2htr in first st, 1dc in next 31 sts, (1dc, 1htr, 1dc) in next st (centre line), 1dc in next 31 sts, 2htr in last st, do not turn, work dc evenly along neck edge, ch8 (buttonhole), sl st in first st to close. Fasten off.

Making up and finishing

Weave in ends and block neatly to finished measurements (see page 123). Sew the button in place (see page 125).

Dino Snood

Beat the cold with a dinosaur-inspired snood. Shaped to fit over the head and around the shoulders, it has the benefit of a hat and a scarf in one. The contrast spikes add a unique character to the design.

SKILL RATING: ● ●

YARN AND MATERIALS

Stylecraft Special Chunky (100% acrylic) chunky (bulky) weight yarn, approx. 144m (157yd) per 100g (3½oz) ball
   1 ball each of:
   Storm Blue 1722 (A)
   Pistachio 1822 (B)

HOOK AND EQUIPMENT

6mm (US size J/10) hook

Stitch markers

Yarn needle

FINISHED MEASUREMENTS

Top of hood to bottom of cowl (excluding spikes): 30.5cm (12in)

Hood top to join in cowl: 19cm (7½in)

Width across cowl (flat at widest part): 28cm (11in)

Hood front to back measures flat 16.5cm (6½in)

TENSION (GAUGE)

11 sts x 6.5 rows measure 10cm (4in) working treble, using 6mm (US size J/10) hook.

ABBREVIATIONS

See page 126.

SPECIAL ABBREVIATION

Ch3 picot: Ch3, sl st in 3rd ch from hook to form a picot point.

Make it yours

This design works with tonal shades for the snood and spikes but you can change up the colours to create your own custom dinosaur.

TIPS The snood portion is worked in rounds; you can use a stitch marker to keep track of the place as you work.

The spikes feature a picot point at the top, these are made by slip stitching back into the first stitch in the chain. Blocking the points will really bring out the shape of the picot.

HOOD

Rejoin A to 1 st after 3rd marker at st 32 from start of round, ch2 (does not count as a st), 1htr in next 33 sts, turn (leave remaining sts unworked). *(33 sts)*
Work on these 33 sts in rows.
Row 1: Ch3 (counts as 1tr throughout), 1tr in each st to end, turn.
Rows 2–12: Ch3, 1tr in each st to end, turn.
Fold in half aligning two raw edges and work 1dc in each of next 16 matching pairs of sts to join two sides, do not turn. Cont down folded centre back of hood and work 15 dc evenly down side of 11 treble rows. *(31 sts total)*
Fasten off.

SPIKES

Join B at front centre top of hood.
Row 1: Ch1 (does not count as a st), 1dc in first st, [miss 2 sts, (4tr, ch3 picot, 4tr) in next st, miss 2 sts, 1dc in next st] 5 times.
Fasten off.

LOWER BORDER

Join in B in any st of bottom edge.
Round 1: Ch1 (does not count as a st throughout), 1dc in each st to end, join with a sl st in first st. *(80 sts)*
Round 2: Ch1, 1dc in first st, miss 1 st, *(4tr, ch3 picot, 4tr) in next st, miss 2 sts, 1dc in next st, miss 2 sts; rep from * to end, join with a sl st in first st.
Fasten off.

FRONT EDGE

Join in B at base of hood on right-hand side.
Round 1: Ch1 (does not count as a st throughout), 66dc evenly around hood and across neckline, join with a sl st in first st. *(66 sts)*
Round 2: Ch1, 1dcBLO in each st to end, join with a sl st in first st.
Fasten off.

Making up and finishing

Weave in all ends and block to shape picot spikes (see page 123).

Snood

Using A, ch80, join with a sl st in first ch to make a ring.
Round 1: Ch1 (does not count as a st), 1dc in each st around, join with a sl st in first st. *(80 sts)*
Place st markers in sts 10, 30, 50 and 70.
Round 2: Ch3 (counts as 1tr throughout), [1tr in each st to 1 st before marked st, tr2tog, 1tr in next st (move marker to st between decreases), tr2tog] 4 times, join with a sl st in top of 3-ch. *(72 sts)*
Round 3: Ch3, [1tr in each st to 2 sts before marked st, tr2tog, 1tr in next st (move marker to st between decreases), tr2tog] 4 times, join with a sl st in top of 3-ch. *(64 sts)*
Round 4: Ch3, [1tr in each st to 2 sts before marked st, tr2tog, 1tr in next st (move marker to st between decreases), tr2tog] 4 times, join with a sl st in top of 3-ch. *(56 sts)*
Round 5: Ch3, [1tr in each st to 2 sts before marked st, tr2tog, 1tr in next st (move marker to st between decreases), tr2tog] 4 times, join with a sl st in top of 3-ch. *(48 sts)*
Rounds 6 and 7: Ch3, 1tr in each st to end (repositioning marker as you work), sl st in first st to join. *(48 sts)*
Fasten off.

Striped Chunky Sweater

Worked in a classic granny stripe stitch pattern, this chunky sweater has a cool retro style. This design is ideal for using up those pretty yarns from your stash.

SKILL RATING: ●●

YARN AND MATERIALS

King Cole Big Value Chunky (100% acrylic) chunky (bulky) weight yarn, approx. 152m (166yd) per 100g (3½oz) ball

  2 balls of Caramel 546 (A)
  1 ball each of:
  Burnt Orange 3491 (B)
  Basil 3489 (light green) (C)
  Turmeric 3486 (yellow) (D)
  Blush 3488 (light pink) (E)

HOOK AND EQUIPMENT

6mm (US size J/10) hook

Stitch markers

Large-eye yarn needle or bodkin

SIZES

3–6 mth: **6–9 mth:** 9–12 mth

FINISHED MEASUREMENTS

3–6 mth: length from shoulder 19cm (7½in), sleeve length from underarm 11cm (4¼in), body circumference 50cm (19¾in)

6–9 mth: length from shoulder 24cm (9½in), sleeve length from underarm 16cm (6¼in), body circumference 55cm (21¾in)

9–12 mth: length from shoulder 29cm (11½in), sleeve length from underarm 16cm (6¼in), body circumference 55cm (21¾in)

TENSION (GAUGE)

Four 3-tr clusters x 8 rows measure 10cm (4in), using 6mm (US size J/10) hook.

ABBREVIATIONS

See page 126.

Sweater

YOKE

Using A, ch40:**48**:56, join with a sl st in first ch to make a ring.

Round 1: Ch1 (does not count as a st throughout), 1htr in each ch to end, join with a sl st in first st. *(40:**48**:56 sts)* Place st markers in sts 9:**9**:9, 15:**15**:19, 29:**33**:37 and 35:**39**:47. Beg of round will be at approx. centre back.

Round 2: Ch3 (counts as 1tr throughout), 1tr in next 2 sts, miss next st, *[1tr in next 3 sts, miss next st] to marked st, (3tr, 1ch, 3tr) in marked st moving marker to 1ch (raglan inc point), miss next st; rep from * three times, [1tr in next 3 sts, miss next st] to end, join with a sl st in top of 3-ch. *(16:**18**:20 3-tr clusters)*

Round 3: Ch3, 2tr in sp at base of 3-ch between clusters, *[3tr in next sp between clusters] to 1-ch sp, (3tr, ch1, 3tr) in 1-ch sp moving marker to 1ch (raglan inc point); rep from * three times, [3tr in next sp between clusters] to end, join with a sl st in top of 3-ch. *(20:**22**:24 3-tr clusters)*

Fasten off A.

. . . .

Make it yours

While this sweater is worked in thin stripes, you could change the design by working two or three rounds before changing colour to make thicker stripes.

. . . .

Round 4: Change to B, ch3, 2tr in sp at base of 3-ch between clusters, *[3tr in next sp between clusters] to 1-ch sp, (3tr, ch1, 3tr) in 1-ch sp moving marker to 1ch (raglan inc point); rep from * three times, [3tr in next sp between clusters] to end, join with a sl st in top of 3-ch. *(24:**26**:28 3-tr clusters)*
Fasten off B.

Round 5: Change to C, ch3, 2tr in sp at base of 3-ch between clusters, *[3tr in next sp between clusters] to 1-ch sp, (3tr, ch1, 3tr) in 1-ch sp moving marker to 1ch (raglan inc point); rep from * three times, [3tr in next sp between clusters] to end, join with a sl st in top of 3-ch. *(28:**30**:32 3-tr clusters)*
Fasten off C.

Round 6: Change to D, ch3, 2tr in sp at base of 3-ch between clusters, *[3tr in next sp between clusters] to 1-ch sp, (3tr, ch1, 3tr) in 1-ch sp moving marker to 1ch (raglan inc point); rep from * three times, [3tr in next sp between clusters] to end, join with a sl st in top of 3-ch. *(32:**34**:36 3-tr clusters)*
Fasten off D.

BODY

Round 7: Change to E, ch3, 2tr in sp at base of 3-ch between clusters, *[3tr in next sp between clusters] to 1-ch sp, 3tr in 1-ch sp, miss next 6:**6**:7) sps, 3tr in next 1-ch sp; rep from * once, [3tr in next sp between clusters] to end, join with a sl st in top of 3-ch. *(20:**22**:22) 3-tr clusters)*
Fasten off E.

Round 8: Change to B, ch3, 2tr in sp at base of 3-ch between clusters, [3tr in next sp between clusters] to end, join with a sl st in top of 3-ch.
Fasten off B.

Round 9: Change to C, ch3, 2tr in sp at base of 3-ch between clusters, [3tr in next sp between clusters] to end, join with a sl st in top of 3-ch.
Fasten off C.

Round 10: Change to D, ch3, 2tr in sp at base of 3-ch between clusters, [3tr in next sp between clusters] to end, join with a sl st in top of 3-ch.
Fasten off D.

Round 11: Change to E, ch3, 2tr in sp at base of 3-ch between clusters, [3tr in next sp between clusters] to end, join with a sl st in top of 3-ch.
Fasten off E.

SIZE 3–6 MTH ONLY

Cont to lower hem.

SIZES 6–9 MTH AND 9–12 MTH ONLY

Rounds 12–15: Rep Rounds 8–11.

SIZE 6–9 MTH ONLY

Cont to lower hem.

SIZE 9–12 MTH ONLY

Rounds 16–19: Rep Rounds 8–11.

ALL SIZES LOWER HEM

Next round: Change to A, ch3, 2tr in sp at base of 3-ch between clusters, [3tr in next sp between clusters] to end, join with a sl st in top of 3-ch.

Next round: Ch3, 2tr in sp at base of 3-ch between clusters, [3tr in next sp between clusters] to end, join with a sl st in top of 3-ch.

Next round: Ch2 (counts as 1htr), 1htr in each st to end, join with a sl st in top of 2-ch. *(60:**66**:66 sts)*

Next round: Ch1, 1dc in each st to end, join with a sl st in first st.
Fasten off.

ALL SIZES SLEEVES

Join in E with sl st in two former raglan inc 1-ch sps at first underarm.

Round 1: Ch3, [3tr in next sp between clusters] to last sp, 2tr in last sp (former raglan inc 1-ch sp), join with a sl st in top of 3-ch. *(7:**7**:8 3-tr clusters)*
Fasten off E.

Round 2: Change to B, ch3, 2tr in sp at base of 3-ch between clusters, [3tr in next sp between clusters] to end, join with a sl st in top of 3-ch.
Fasten off B.

Round 3: Change to C, ch3, 2tr in sp at base of 3-ch between clusters, [3tr in next sp between clusters] to end, join with a sl st in top of 3-ch.
Fasten off C.

Round 4: Change to D, ch3, 2tr in sp at base of 3-ch between clusters, [3tr in next sp between clusters] to end, join with a sl st in top of 3-ch.
Fasten off D.

Round 5: Change to E, ch3, 2tr in sp at base of 3-ch between clusters, [3tr in next sp between clusters] to end, join with a sl st in top of 3-ch.
Fasten off E.

SIZE 3–6 MTH ONLY

Cont to cuff.

SIZES 6–9 MTH AND 9–12 MTH ONLY

Rounds 6–9: Rep Rounds 2–5.

ALL SIZES CUFFS

Next round: Change to A, ch3, 2tr in sp at base of 3-ch between clusters, [3tr in next sp between clusters] to end, join with a sl st in top of 3-ch.

Next round: Ch3, 2tr in sp at base of 3-ch between clusters, [3tr in next sp between clusters] to end, join with a sl st in top of 3-ch.

Next round: Ch2 (counts as 1htr), 1htr in each st to end, join with a sl st in top of 2-ch. *(21:**21**:24 sts)*

Next round: Ch1 (does not count as st), 1dc in each st to end, join with a sl st in first st.
Fasten off A.
Rep sleeve and cuff on other side.

Making up and finishing

Weave in all ends and block neatly to measurements (see page 123).

TIPS This sweater is worked from the top down, meaning that you can do a fit-check as you work by slipping it onto the recipient. You can then increase or decrease the length of the sleeves or body by working more or fewer rounds.

This sweater uses chunky yarn; you may find that you need a really large-eye yarn needle or bodkin to weave the ends in during the finishing.

Unisex Romper

This crochet romper is cute and colourful. Based around a classic dungaree design, it is worked from the legs up and finished with simple button-up straps.

SKILL RATING: ● ●

YARN AND MATERIALS

Stylecraft Special DK (100% acrylic) DK (light worsted) weight yarn, approx. 295m (323yd) per 3½oz (100g) ball
1 ball each of:
Mushroom 1832 (light brown) (A)
Wisteria 1432 (mauve) (B)
Cloud Blue 1019 (C)
Spring Green 1316 (D)
Lemon 1020 (E)
Apricot 1026 (F)
Pale Rose 1080 (G)

2 buttons, 1.5cm (⅝in) diameter

HOOK AND EQUIPMENT

4mm (US size G/6) hook

Stitch markers

Yarn needle

SIZES

3–6 mth: **6–9 mth:** 9–12 mth

FINISHED MEASUREMENTS

3–6 mth: length 34.5cm (13½in), body circumference 39cm (15½in)

6–9 mth: length 37.5cm (14¾in), body circumference 43cm (17in)

9–12 mth: length 41cm (16in), body circumference 50cm (20in)

Straps: width 4cm (1½in), length 18cm (7in)

TENSION (GAUGE)

18 sts x 13 rows measure 10cm (4in) working half treble, using 4mm (US size G/6) hook.

ABBREVIATIONS

See page 126.

Romper

CUFFS

(make 2)
Using A, ch5.
Row 1: 1dc in 2nd ch from hook, 1dc in each ch to end, turn. *(4 sts)*
Row 2: Ch1 (does not count as a st throughout), 1dcBLO in each dc to end, turn.
Rep Row 2 a further 28:**32**:38 times. *(30:**34**:40 rows in total)*
Fold work in half across width aligning current row with foundation chain. Join with a sl st to make a round (cuff will be closed later).
Turn work onto side so you are working into row ends, ch1, 1dc in end of each row, join with a sl st in first st. *(30:**34**:40 sts)*
Begin working in rounds.

· ·

Make it yours

This design is worked in repeated stripes – change the look by working in two shades or increase the number of rows between the colour changes for chunky blocks of colour.

· ·

Next round: Ch2 (counts as 1htr throughout), 1htr in next 5:**6**:8 sts, 2htr in next st, *1htr in next 6:**7**:9 sts, 2htr in next st; rep from * to last 2:**2**:0 sts, 1htr in last 2:**2**:0 sts, join with a sl st in top of 2-ch. *(34:**38**:44 sts)*

Next round: Change to B, ch2, 1htr in next 6:**7**:9 sts, 2htr in next st, *1htr in next 7:**8**:10 sts, 2htr in next st; rep from * to last 2:**2**:0 sts, 1htr in last 2:**2**:0 sts, join with a sl st in top of 2-ch. *(38:**42**:48 sts)*

Next round: Change to C, ch2, 1htr in next 7:**8**:10 sts, 2htr in next st, *1htr in next 8:**9**:11 sts, 2htr in next st; rep from * to last 2:**2**:0 sts, 1htr in last 2:**2**:0 sts, join with a sl st in top of 2-ch. *(42:**46**:52 sts)*

Next round: Change to D, ch2, 1htr in each st to end, join with a sl st in top of 2-ch.

Next round: Change to E, ch2, 1htr in each st to end, join with a sl st in top of 2-ch.

Next round: Change to F, ch2, 1htr in each st to end, join with a sl st in top of 2-ch.

Next round: Change to G, ch2, 1htr in each st to end, join with a sl st in top of 2-ch.

JOIN CROTCH

Mark 10 sts on each leg piece.
Using G, work 1dc in each marked st on leg one, turn. Now work in rows.

Row 1: Ch2, 1htr in next 10 sts, turn.
Row 2: Ch1, 1dc in next 10 sts and join them to 10 marked dc along second leg, matching st to st. Fasten off.

BODY

Join B at centre back of one leg, ch2 (counts as 1htr throughout), 1htr in each st around both legs working 3 sts across each side of crotch seam. *(70:**78**:90 sts)*
Now cont working in rounds.

Round 1: Change to C, ch2, 1htr in each st to end, join with a sl st in top of 2-ch.
Rep Round 1 a further 14:**18**:22 times, changing colour with each round as set.

Next round: Change to A, ch2, 1htr in next 4:**3**:6 sts, htr2tog, *1htr in next 5:**6**:7 sts, htr2tog; rep from * to end, join with a sl st in top of 2-ch. *(60:**68**:80 sts)*

Next round: Ch2, 1htr in each st to end, join with a sl st in top of 2-ch.

Next round: Ch2, 1htr in next 3:**2**:5 sts, htr2tog, *1htr in next 4:**5**:6 sts, htr2tog; rep from * to end, join with a sl st in top of 2-ch. *(50:**58**:70 sts)*

Next round: Ch2, 1htr in each st to end, join with a sl st in top of 2-ch.

Next round: Ch2, 1htr in next 2:**1**:4 sts, htr2tog, *1htr in next 3:**4**:5 sts, htr2tog; rep from * to end, join with a sl st in top of 2-ch. *(40:**48**:60 sts)*

Fasten off.

FRONT BIB

Mark 26:**28**:30 sts along centre front of garment and beg working in rows.

Row 1 (RS): Join A at beg of marked sts, ch1 (does not count as a st throughout), 1dc in next 6 sts, 1htr in next 14:**16**:18 sts, 1dc in next 6 sts, turn. *(26:**28**:30 sts)*

Row 2: Ch1, skip first st, 1dc in next 5 sts, 1htr in next 14:**16**:18 sts, 1dc in next 5 sts, turn. *(24:**26**:28 sts)*

Row 3: Ch1, skip first st, 1dc in next 4 sts, 1htr in next 14:**16**:18 sts, 1dc in next 4 sts, turn. *(22:**24**:26 sts)*

Row 4: Ch1, skip first st, 1dc in next 3 sts, 1htr in next 14:**16**:18 sts, 1dc in next 3 sts, turn. *(20:**22**:24 sts)*

Row 5: Ch1, skip first st, 1dc in next 2 sts, 1htr in next 14:**16**:18 sts, 1dc in next 2 sts, turn. *(18:**20**:22 sts)*

Row 6: Ch1, skip first st, 1dc in st, 1htr in next 14:**16**:18 sts, 1dc in next st, turn. *(16:**18**:20 sts)*

Row 7: Ch2 (does not count as a st), skip first st, 1htr in next 14:**16**:18 sts, turn. *(14:**16**:18 sts)*

Row 8: Ch2, skip first st, 1htr in next 12:**14**:16 sts, skip last st. *(12:**14**:16 sts)*

Fasten off.

STRAPS

Find centre back point and mark two sets of 5 sts spaced 2:**4**:6 sts apart at centre back.

Row 1 (RS): Join A at beg of first set of marked sts, ch1 (does not count as a st), 1dc in each st, turn. *(5 sts)*

Row 2: Ch2 (counts as 1htr throughout), 1htr in each st to end, turn.

Rep Row 2 a further 18 times.

Next row (buttonhole): Ch2, 1htr in next st, miss next st, ch1, 1htr in last 2 sts, turn.

Next row: Ch2, 1htr in each st to end, turn. *(5 sts)*

Rep last row twice more.

Fasten off.

Rep on second set of marked sts to create second strap. Join A in any st of body and work a round of dc evenly around entire edge of upper body and straps, join with a sl st in first st. Fasten off.

Making up and finishing

Weave in all ends and block neatly as desired (see page 123). Sew on the buttons to the front of the romper, ensuring that they are affixed securely (see page 125).

TIPS Stitch markers are a handy way to keep track of the start of each round.

When sewing on the buttons be sure that they are stitched on securely so as not to pose a hazard to babies and small children.

Toddler Poncho

With just the right amount of retro charm this colourful striped poncho will give boho-vibes and add a cosy layer to little bodies. Plus, its simple shape is easy to customise to any size you like!

SKILL RATING: ●●

YARN AND MATERIALS

James C Brett Top Value DK (100% acrylic) DK (light worsted) weight yarn, approx. 290m (317yd) per 100g (3½oz) ball

1 ball each of:
Parchment 843 (grey) (A)
Lilac 8431 (B)
Baby Blue 8418 (C)
Fondant 8463 (pink) (D)
Mint 8413 (light turquoise) (E)

HOOK AND EQUIPMENT

4mm (US size G/6) hook
Stitch markers (optional)
Yarn needle

SIZES

12–18 mth: **18–24 mth:** 24–36 mth

FINISHED MEASUREMENTS

12–18 mth: neckline to point 25.5cm (10in), neck circumference 32.5cm (13in)

18–24 mth: neckline to point 30.5cm (12in), neck circumference 36.5cm (14½in)

24–36 mth: neckline to point 35.5cm (14in), neck circumference 40.5cm (16in)

TENSION (GAUGE)

Five 3-tr clusters x 8 rows measure 10cm (4in), using 4mm (US size G/6) hook.

ABBREVIATIONS

See page 126.

Poncho

Using A, ch64:**72**:80, join with a sl st in first ch to make a ring.

Round 1: Ch3 (counts as 1tr throughout), 1tr in next 2 sts, [ch1, miss next st, 1tr in next 3 sts] 15:**17**:19 times, ch1, miss next st, sl st in first st to join.
*(16:**18**:20 tr clusters)*
Fasten off A.

Round 2: Join in B, ch3, 2tr in ch sp at base of 3-ch, [ch1, 3tr in next ch sp] 7:**8**:9 times, ch1, (3tr, ch1, 3tr) in next ch sp, [ch1, 3tr in next ch sp] 7:**8**:9 times, ch1, 3tr in last ch sp, ch1, join with a sl st in top of 3-ch.
*(18:**20**:22 tr clusters)*
Fasten off B.

. . . .

Make it yours

This design is worked from a foundation chain length that is a multiple of eight stitches. You can create any size poncho by lengthening the foundation chain by multiples of eight until it fits over the head or is equal to the head circumference – ideal for a mummy and me project! To lengthen the poncho, work additional rounds before the Lower Border.

. . . .

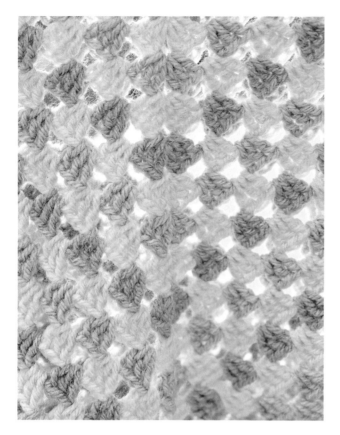

TIPS To keep the colour changes neat, fasten off the yarns securely after each round to add in the next colour. You can hold the yarn tails against the inside of the work and use the working yarn to secure them as you make the stitches in the next round.

Once the first few rounds of the poncho have been worked the pattern has been established and will be easier to follow. You may like to use stitch markers to mark the increase points to help keep you on track.

Round 3: Join in C, ch3, 2tr in ch sp at base of 3-ch, [ch1, 3tr in next ch sp] 8:**9**:10 times, ch1, (3tr, ch1, 3tr) in next ch sp, [ch1, 3tr in next ch sp] 8:**9**:10 times, ch1, 3tr in last ch sp, ch1, join with a sl st in top of 3-ch. *(20:**22**:24 tr clusters)*
Fasten off C.
Round 4: Join in D, ch3, 2tr in ch sp at base of 3-ch, [ch1, 3tr in next ch sp] 9:**10**:11 times, ch1, (3tr, ch1, 3tr) in next ch sp, [ch1, 3tr in next ch sp] 9:**10**:11 times, ch1, 3tr in last ch sp, ch1, join with a sl st in top of 3-ch. *(22:**24**:26 tr clusters)*
Fasten off D.
Round 5: Join in E, ch3, 2tr in ch sp at base of 3-ch, [ch1, 3tr in next ch sp] 10:**11**:12 times, ch1, (3tr, ch1, 3tr) in next ch sp, [ch1, 3tr in next ch sp] 10:**11**:12 times, ch1, 3tr in last ch sp, ch1, join with a sl st in top of 3-ch. *(24:**26**:28 tr clusters)*
Fasten off E.
Cont in pattern as set for a further 8:**12**:16 rows, working in stripes of B, C, D and E, increasing at each side and working one more 3-tr cluster on front and back with each row. *(40:**50**:60 tr clusters)*
Join in A and work 2 more rows in pattern with A only. Do not fasten off. *(44:**54**:64 tr clusters)*

LOWER BORDER
Round 1: Ch1 (does not count as a st throughout), 1dc in each st and ch sp around, join with a sl st in first st. *(176:**216**:256 sts)*
Round 2: Ch2 (counts as 1htr), 1htr in each st around, join with a sl st in top of 2-ch.
Round 3: Ch1, 1dc in each st around, join with a sl st in first st.
Fasten off.

NECKLINE
Join in A in any st of foundation chain.
Round 1: Ch1 (does not count as a st throughout), 1dc in each foundation ch around neckline, join with a sl st in first st. *(64:**72**:80 sts)*
Round 2: Ch2 (counts as 1htr), 1htr in each st around, join with a sl st in top of 2-ch.
Round 3: Ch1, 1dc in each st around, join with a sl st in first st.
Fasten off.

Making up and finishing
Weave in all ends neatly and block to measurements (see page 123).

Lace Dress

The lacy stitch on the dress creates a pretty shell motif which is gathered into a simple bodice. Worked in a rainbow variegated yarn, this dress is perfect for parties or special occasions.

SKILL RATING: ● ● ●

YARN AND MATERIALS

James C Brett Shhh (80% acrylic, 20% wool) DK (light worsted) weight yarn, approx. 550m (599yd) per 100g (3½oz) ball
   1 ball of SH05 (multi pastels)

2 small buttons

HOOK AND EQUIPMENT

4mm (US size G/6) hook

Stitch marker

Yarn needle

SIZES

9–12 mth: **12–18 mth:** 18–24 mth

FINISHED MEASUREMENTS

9–12 mth: bodice width 20.5cm (8in), skirt length 25.5cm (10in)

12–18 mth: bodice width 23cm (9in), skirt length 32cm (12½in)

18–24 mth: bodice width 25.5cm (10in), skirt length 38cm (15in)

TENSION (GAUGE)

Each two-row shell measures 5cm (2in) wide by 3cm (1¼in) tall, using 4mm (US size G/6) hook.

ABBREVIATIONS

See page 126.

Make it yours

Variegated yarn is perfect for creating colourful garments. To change up the look, pick a solid shade yarn for the bodice to create a contrast.

BODICE SIZE 9–12 MTH ONLY

With RS facing, join yarn to top edge of skirt, 1dc in each st along foundation ch, join with a sl st in first st. *(140 sts)*

Round 1: [1htr in next st, htr2tog] 10 times, [1htr in next 2 sts, htr2tog] 20 times, [1htr in next st, htr2tog] 10 times. *(100 sts)*

Work in a continuous spiral, placing marker for start of round.

Round 2: [1htr in next 2 sts, htr2tog] 25 times. *(75 sts)*

Round 3: [1htr in next st, htr2tog] 25 times. *(50 sts)*

Rounds 4–6: 1htr in each st to end.

Rounds 7–11: 1htr in next 8 sts, sl st in next 8 sts, 1htr in next 18 sts, sl st in next 8 sts, 1htr in next 8 sts.

Round 12: 1dc in next 8 sts, sl st in next 8 sts, 1dc in next 18 sts, sl st in next 8 sts, 1dc in next 8 sts. Fasten off.

BODICE SIZE 12–18 MTH ONLY

With RS facing, join yarn to top edge of skirt, 1dc in each st along foundation ch, join with a sl st in first st. *(150 sts)*

Round 1: [1htr in next st, htr2tog] 50 times. *(100 sts)*

Work in a continuous spiral, placing marker for start of round.

Round 2: [1htr in next 2 sts, htr2tog] 25 times. *(75 sts)*

Round 3: [1htr in next 3 sts, htr2tog] 15 times. *(60 sts)*

Rounds 4–7: 1htr in each st to end

Rounds 9–14: 1htr in next 10 sts, sl st in next 10 sts, 1htr in next 20 sts, sl st in next 10 sts, 1htr in next 10 sts.

Round 15: 1dc in next 10 sts, sl st in next 10 sts, 1dc in next 20 sts, sl st in next 10 sts, 1dc in next 10 sts. Fasten off.

BODICE SIZE 18–24 MTH ONLY

With RS facing, join yarn to top edge of skirt, 1dc in each st along foundation ch, join with a sl st in first st. *(160 sts)*

Round 1: [1htr in next 3 sts, htr2tog] 10 times, [1htr in next 4 sts, htr2tog] 10 times, [1htr in next 3 sts, htr2tog] 10 times. *(130 sts)*

Work in a continuous spiral, placing marker for start of round.

Round 2: [1htr in next 2 sts, htr2tog] 10 times, [1tr in next 3 sts, htr2tog] 10 times, [1htr in next 2 sts, htr2tog] 10 times. *(100 sts)*

Round 3: [1htr in next 2 sts, htr2tog] 25 times. *(75 sts)*

Rounds 4–8: 1htr in each st to end.

Rounds 9–14: 1htr in next 12 sts, sl st in next 13 sts, 1htr in next 25 sts, sl st in next 13 sts, 1htr in next 12 sts.

Round 15: 1dc in next 12 sts, sl st in next 13 sts, 1dc in next 25 sts, sl st in next 13 sts, 1dc in next 12 sts. Fasten off.

Dress

SKIRT

Ch141:**151**:161.

Row 1 (WS): 1dc in 2nd ch from hook and each ch to end, turn. *(140:**150**:160 sts)*

Row 2 (RS): Ch1 (does not count as a st throughout), 1dc, *miss 4 sts, 9dtr in next st, miss 4 sts, 1dc in next st; rep from * to end, turn.

Row 3: Ch4 (counts as 1 dtr), 1dtr in same st, *ch3, miss 4 dtr, 1dc in next dtr, ch3, miss 4 dtr, 2dtr in next dc; rep from * to end, turn.

Row 4: Ch1, 1dc in sp between next 2 dtr, *miss 3 ch, 9dtr in next dc, miss 3 ch, 1dc in sp between next 2 dtr; rep from * to end working last dc in 4-ch sp, turn.

Rep Rows 3 and 4 a further 6:**8**:10 times, or to desired length.

There are 8 shell rows for 9–12m size, 10 shell rows for 12–18m size and 12 shell rows for 18–24m size. Fasten off.

Straps

(make 2)
Ch6.
Row 1: 1dc in 2nd from hook and each ch to end. *(5 sts)*
Row 2: Ch1 (does not count as a st), 1dc in each st to end, turn.
Rep Row 2 until strap measures 12.5–15cm (5–6in) as desired.
Fasten off.

Making up and finishing

Weave in ends and block neatly to finished measurements (see page 123).
Sew the centre back seam of the skirt.
Place the straps onto the top of the back bodice and sew into position. Bring the straps to the front and sew in place. Sew the buttons into place to finish (see page 125).

TIPS The straps feature faux buttons, meaning that you can set the straps to the suitable size for the child and sew in place.

The lace is worked over a two-row repeat, and features double trebles, an elongated stitch. Once a few rows have been worked the pattern of the lace has been set and it is easier to follow.

SKILL RATING: ●

YARN AND MATERIALS

Sirdar Happy Cotton (100% cotton) DK (light worsted) weight yarn, approx. 43m (47yd) per 20g (¾oz) ball

1 ball each of:
Sundae 787 (pale yellow) (A)
Freckle 753 (orange) (B)
Flamingo 760 (pink) (C)
Fizz 779 (green) (D)

Plastic child's headband

HOOK AND EQUIPMENT

4mm (US size G/6) hook

Yarn needle

FINISHED MEASUREMENTS

Each flower measures 4.5cm (1¾in) across

TENSION (GAUGE)

Not applicable for this project.

ABBREVIATIONS

See page 126.

Floral Headband

Quick and easy colourful flowers make the perfect accessory. This trio of blooms makes a pretty accent, or opt for a full headband of flowers for a Frida Kahlo-style version.

Flower

(make 3, 1 each in A, B and C)
Using A, ch32.
Row 1: 1dc in 2nd ch from hook, *ch2, skip 1 ch, 1dc in next ch; rep from * to end, turn. *(15 ch sps)*
Row 2: Ch2, (4htr, ch1, sl st) in first ch sp, [(sl st, ch1, 4 htr, ch 1, sl st) in next ch sp] 4 times (5 small petals created), [(sl st, ch1, 4tr, ch1, sl st) in next ch sp] 10 times (10 large petals created). *(15 petals)*
Fasten off, leaving a long yarn tail.
With smaller petals in the centre, roll strip to make a flower. Use yarn tail to secure flower at base.

Headband

Using D, ch 7.
Row 1: 1dc in 2nd ch from hook and each st to end, turn. *(6 sts)*
Rows 2–10: Ch1 (does not count as a st throughout), 1dc in each st to end, turn.
Row 11: Ch1, 2dc in first st, 1dc in next 4 sts, 2 dc in last st, turn. *(8 sts)*
Rows 12–46: Ch1, 1dc in each st to end, turn.
Row 47: Ch1, dc2tog, 1dc in next 4 sts, dc2tog, turn. *(6 sts)*
Rows 48–58: Ch1, 1dc in each st to end, turn.
Fasten off, leaving a long yarn tail.

Making up and finishing

Place the headband piece around the headband and seam together securely along the inside of the headband. Place the three flowers into position on the headband and use the yarn tails to sew into place securely.

Make it yours

Add a contrast edge to the flower by working a row of slip stitches around the completed petals before securing in place.

TIPS Leaving longer yarn tails at the start and end of the flower will give enough yarn to secure the petals when rolling up, and also some yarn to secure the flower to the headband.

The headband piece is worked flat and seamed – this means that you can check how the size fits against your headband. You can make the piece wider by increasing stitches or narrower by decreasing stitches. The strips need to be long enough to wrap around the headband and be seamed into position.

Toddler Tunic

This over-size tunic is great for keeping busy toddlers cosy. The simple, slip-on tabard design is quick and easy to make and features spike stitches for added detail on the colour changes.

SKILL RATING: ●

YARN AND MATERIALS

Sirdar Hayfield Bonus Aran (100% acrylic) aran (worsted) weight yarn, approx. 256m (280yd) per 100g (3½oz) ball
1 ball each of:
Birch 580 (cream) (A)
Frost Blue 608 (pale blue) (B)
Lavender 565 (pale lavender) (C)
Lagoon Blue 607 (green) (D)

HOOK AND EQUIPMENT

5mm (US size H/8) hook

Yarn needle

SIZES

9–18 mth: **18–24 mth:** 24–36 mth

FINISHED MEASUREMENTS

9–18 mth: 28 x 35.5cm (11 x 14in)

18–24 mth: 30.5 x 40.5cm (12 x 16in)

24–36 mth: 33 x 45.75cm (13 x 18in)

TENSION (GAUGE)

15 sts x 17 rows measure 10cm (4in) working double crochet, using 5mm (US size H/8) hook.

ABBREVIATIONS

See page 126.

Tunic

(make 2 the same, front and back)
Using A, ch31:**36**:41.
Row 1: 1dc in 2nd ch from hook and each ch to end, turn. *(30:**35**:40 sts)*
Rows 2–5: Ch1 (does not count as a st throughout), 1dc in each st to end, turn.

Make it yours

This design works with a four-shade colour pattern repeat, but you can add in more colours or alternate between two shades to change the look.

Row 6 (spike st): Change to B, *1dc in next st one row below, 1dc in next st on second row below, 1dc in next st on third row below, 1dc in next st on second row below, 1dc in next st one row below; rep from * to end, turn.
Rows 7–11: Ch1, 1dc in each st to end, turn.
Row 12 (spike st): Change to C, *1dc in next st one row below, 1dc in next st on second row below, 1dc in next st on third row below, 1dc in next st on second row below, 1dc in next st one row below; rep from * to end, turn.
Rows 13–17: Ch1, 1dc in each st to end, turn.
Row 18 (spike st): Change to D, *1dc in next st one row below, 1dc in next st on second row below, 1dc in next st on third row below, 1dc in next st on second row below, 1dc in next st one row below; rep from * to end, turn.
Cont in patt as set, finishing on Rows 59:**65**:71.
Fasten off.

BORDER

Worked on each side and neckline edge in turn.
Row 1: Join B in corner, ch3 (counts as 1tr throughout), 1tr in each row end down side of tunic, turn.
Row 2: Ch3, 1tr in each st to end.
Fasten off.
Rep for opposite side, then rep for neckline edge, working 1tr in each st and 2tr in each row end of side borders.

BOTTOM BORDER

Row 1: Join B in corner, ch3 (counts as 1tr), 1tr in each st to end.
Fasten off.

Making up and finishing

Place the front and back panels with RS together and WS facing. Create the side seams by threading B onto a yarn needle and sewing a seam for 20.5–30.5cm (8–12in) (to suit the child you're making the tunic for) up from the lower hem, leaving an opening at the top for the armhole.
Fasten off.
Repeat on the second side.
Create the neckline seam by threading a yarn needle with B and sewing a seam for 10–13cm (4–5in) (to suit the child you're making the tunic for) in from each side towards the neckline, leaving an opening in the middle.
Fasten off and weave in all ends (see page 123).

TIPS When working the spike stitches, be sure not to pull the yarn loops that are worked through the lower stitches too tight because this can gather up the work.

The front and the back are worked in the same manner – be sure that the wrong sides are facing when they are seamed together for the best finish.

Head Warmer

This crochet headband is perfect for keeping little ones warm when the temperature drops – and a great alternative for those toddlers who simply don't keep hats on!

SKILL RATING: ●

YARN AND MATERIALS

Berroco Ultra Alpaca (50% alpaca, 50% wool) aran (worsted) weight yarn, approx. 200m (219yd) per 100g (3½oz) ball
1 ball each of:
Zephyr 62111 (pale turquoise) (A)
Tea Rose 62114 (pale pink) (B)

HOOK AND EQUIPMENT

5.5mm (US size I/9) hook

Yarn needle

FINISHED MEASUREMENTS

41 x 8.5cm (16 x 3¼in)

TENSION (GAUGE)

16 sts x 10 rows measure 10cm (4in) working half treble, using 5.5mm (US size I/9) hook.

ABBREVIATIONS

See page 126.

Head warmer

Using A, ch55.
Row 1: 1dc in 2nd ch from hook and each ch to end, turn. *(54 sts)*
Row 2: Change to B, ch2 (counts as 1htr throughout), 1htr in each st to end, turn.
Row 3: Ch2, 1htr in each st to end, turn.
Row 4: Change to A, ch1 (does not count as a st throughout), 1dc in each st to end, turn.
Rows 5 and 6: Change to B, ch2, 1htr in each st to end, turn.
Row 7: Change to A, ch1, 1dc in each st to end, turn.
Rep Rows 5–7 once more.
Fasten off, leaving a long yarn tail for seaming.

Band

Using B, ch6.
Row 1: 1dc in 2nd ch from hook and each ch to end, turn. *(5 sts)*
Row 2: Ch1 (does not count as a st), 1dc in each st to end, turn.
Rep Row 2 ten more times.
Fasten off, leaving a long yarn tail for seaming.

Making up and finishing

Align the short edges of the head warmer and sew together, drawing the yarn in to gather up. Wrap the band around the gathered join in the head warmer and seam in place to cover the join. Weave in all ends (see page 123).

TIPS The head warmer size can be customized by either increasing the number of chain stitches in the foundation chain or decreasing for a larger or smaller size.

Leaving longer yarn ends when fastening off will make the finishing stages quicker as you can use these for joining the seams for each of the pieces.

Make it yours

Create a chunkier head warmer by increasing the width; once gathered this will give a wider section to cover the head and ears.

Rainbow Cardi

This cropped cardigan is a cute cover-up for boys and girls. Worked in single row stripes, this project is ideal for using up all the leftover yarn in your stash.

SKILL RATING: ● ●

YARN AND MATERIALS

Stylecraft Special DK (100% acrylic) DK (light worsted) weight yarn, approx. 295m (323yd) per 100g (3½oz) ball
  1 ball each of:
    Pomegranate 1083 (deep pink) (A)
    Vintage Peach 1836 (peach) (B)
    Buttermilk 1835 (pale yellow) (C)
    Lincoln 1834 (green) (D)
    Cloud Blue 1019 (pale blue) (E)
    Lavender 1188 (F)
    Grape 1067 (purple) (G)
    Pale Rose 1080 (pink) (H)

3 buttons

HOOK AND EQUIPMENT

4mm (US size G/6) hook

4 stitch markers

Yarn needle

SIZES

9–12 mth: **12–18 mth:** 18–24 mth

FINISHED MEASUREMENTS

9–12 mth: back neck to hem 18cm (7in), across chest 24cm (9½in), sleeve length 13cm (5¼in)

12–18 mth: back neck to hem 20.5cm (8in), across chest 24cm (9½in), sleeve length 13cm (5¼in)

18–24 mth: back neck to hem 24cm (9½in), across chest 24cm (9½in), sleeve length 16.5cm (6½in)

TENSION (GAUGE)

17 sts x 12 rows measure 10cm (4in) working half treble, using 4mm (US size G/6) hook.

ABBREVIATIONS

See page 126.

Yoke

Using A, ch53:**69**:77
Row 1: 1dc in 2nd ch from hook and each ch to end, turn. (52:**68**:76 sts)

SIZE 9–12M ONLY

Row 2: Ch1 (does not count as a st), 1dc in each st to end, placing markers in 7th, 20th, 33rd and 46th sts. Front 6 sts (marker), sleeve 12 sts (marker), back 12 sts (marker), sleeve 12 sts (marker), front 6 sts.

SIZE 12–18M ONLY

Row 2: Ch1 (does not count as a st), 1dc in each st to end, placing markers in 9th, 26th, 43rd and 60th sts. Front 8 sts (marker), sleeve 16 sts (marker), back 16 sts (marker), sleeve 16 sts (marker), front 8 sts.

SIZE 18–24M ONLY

Row 2: Ch1 (does not count as a st), 1dc in each st to end, placing markers in 10th, 29th, 48th and 67th sts. Front 9 sts (marker), sleeve 18 sts (marker), back 18 sts (marker), sleeve 18 sts (marker), front 9 sts.

ALL SIZES

Inc will be worked in marked sts.
Row 3: Change to B, ch2 (does not count as a st throughout), [1htr in each st to marked st, (1htr, ch2, 1htr) in marked st] 4 times, 1htr in each st to end, turn. (56:**72**:80 sts)
Row 4: Change to C, ch2, [1htr in each st to ch sp, (1htr, ch2, 1htr) in ch sp] 4 times, 1htr in each st to end, turn. (64:**80**:88 sts)
Row 5: Change to D, [1htr in each st to ch sp, (1htr, ch2, 1htr) in ch sp] 4 times, 1htr in each st to end, turn. (72:**88**:96 sts)
Row 6: Change to E, ch2, [1htr in each st to ch sp, (1htr, ch2, 1htr) in ch sp] 4 times, 1htr in each st to end, turn. (80:**96**:104 sts)
Row 7: Change to F, ch2, [1htr in each st to ch sp, (1htr, ch2, 1htr) in ch sp] 4 times, 1htr in each st to end, turn. (88:**104**:112 sts)

Make it yours

This cardigan features a repeated colour pattern, but you can use any shades you like – mix and match from your stash for a really unique garment.

Row 8: Change to G, ch2, [1htr in each st to ch sp, (1htr, ch2, 1htr) in ch sp] 4 times, 1htr in each st to end, turn. (96:**112**:120 sts)
Row 9: Change to H, ch2, [1htr in each st to ch sp, (1htr, ch2, 1htr) in ch sp] 4 times, 1htr in each st to end, turn. (104:**120**:128 sts)
Cont to change colour every row as set.
Row 10: Ch2, [1htr in each st to ch sp, (1htr, ch2, 1htr) in ch sp] 4 times, 1htr in each st to end, turn. (112:**128**:136 sts)
Row 11: Ch2, [1htr in each st to ch sp, (1htr, ch2, 1htr) in ch sp] 4 times, 1htr in each st to end, turn. (120:**136**:144 sts)

SIZES 12–18 MTH AND 18–24 MTH ONLY

Row 12: Ch2, [1htr in each st to ch sp, (1htr, ch2, 1htr) in ch sp] 4 times, 1htr in each st to end, turn. (**144**:152 sts)

SIZE 18–24 MTH ONLY

Row 13: Ch2, [1htr in each st to ch sp, (1htr, ch2, 1htr) in ch sp] 4 times, 1htr in each st to end, turn. *(160 sts)*

BODY SIZE 9–12 MTH ONLY

Next row: Ch2, 1htr in next 15 sts, 1htr in ch sp, miss next 30 sts, 1htr in ch sp, 1htr in next 30 sts, 1htr in ch sp, miss next 30 sts, 1htr in ch sp, 1htr in next 15 sts. *(64 sts)*

Cont working on these 64 sts.

BODY SIZE 12–18 MTH ONLY

Next row: Ch2, 1htr in next 18 sts, 1htr in ch sp, miss next 36 sts, 1htr in ch sp, 1htr in next 36 sts, 1htr in ch sp, miss next 36 sts, 1htr in ch sp, 1htr in next 18 sts. *(76 sts)*

Cont working on these 76 sts.

BODY SIZE 18–24 MTH ONLY

Next row: Ch2, 1htr in next 20 sts, 1htr in ch sp, miss next 40 sts, 1htr in ch sp, 1htr in next 40 sts, 1htr in ch sp, miss next 40 sts, 1htr in ch sp, 1htr in next 20 sts. *(84 sts)*

Cont working on these 84 sts.

ALL SIZES

Next row: Ch2, 1htr in each st to end, turn.

Cont working in rows on these 76:**64**:84 sts, changing colour on each new row until work measures 18:**20.5**:24cm (7:**8**:9½in) from back neck to hem.

Fasten off.

SLEEVES

Following yarn order as set, join in next colour at any point on sleeve, ch2 (counts as 1htr throughout), 1htr in each st around, working 2htr in st at centre of armpit, join with a sl st in top of 2-ch. *(31:**37**:41 sts)*

Next round: Ch2, 1htr in each st to end, join with a sl st in top of 2-ch.

Cont working in rounds on these 31:**37**:41 sts, changing colour on each new round until sleeve measures 13:**13**:16.5cm (5¼:**5¼**:6½in) from neck edge, or desired length.

Fasten off.

Repeat for second sleeve.

Making up and finishing

Weave in all ends and block neatly to finished measurements (see page 123). Place three buttons onto chosen side and sew into place (see page 125).

BORDER

With RS facing, join A in any st at neckline, ch1 (does not count as a st), 1dc in each st around entire outer edge of garment, making buttonhole with ch3–6 (depending on size of button) opposite buttons at front, then cont to work 1dc in each st to end, join with a sl st in first st. Fasten off.

SLEEVE BORDER

Join A in any st at base of sleeve, ch1 (does not count as a st), 1dc in each st around, join with a sl st in first st. Fasten off and repeat for second sleeve. Weave in all ends.

TIPS This cardigan is worked from the top down, crocheting the yoke first and then setting aside stitches for both sleeves, before working the lower body.

The buttonholes are made with chain stitches – you can make these to suit your button size. Simply increase the chain length for larger buttons and reduce for smaller buttons.

chapter 2

Nursery & Blankets

Star Garland

Add a dreamy accent to a nursery or child's bedroom with this star garland, created with coloured tassels and crochet stars.

SKILL RATING: ● ●

YARN AND MATERIALS

Paintbox Yarns Cotton DK (100% cotton) DK (light worsted) weight yarn, approx. 125m (137yd) per 50g (¾oz) ball
   1 ball each of:
   Mustard Yellow 424 (A)
   Kingfisher Blue 435 (turquoise) (B)
   Dolphin Blue 437 (C)

Approx. 200cm (79in) of grey T-shirt yarn or thick cord

30 wooden beads, 20mm (¾in) size

HOOK AND EQUIPMENT

4mm (US size G/6) hook

7.5 x 15cm (3 x 6in) piece of card

FINISHED MEASUREMENTS

156cm (61½in) long

TENSION (GAUGE)

Not important in this project.

ABBREVIATIONS

See page 126.

Stars

(make 7)
Using A, make a magic ring.
Round 1: Ch3 (counts as first tr), 9tr in ring, join with a sl st in 3rd of 3-ch. *(10 sts)*
Round 2: Ch1 (does not count as a st), [1dc in next st, (1tr, 1dtr, ch1, 1dtr, 1tr) in next st] 4 times, join with a sl st to first st.
Fasten off, leaving a long yarn tail. Block neatly (see page 123).

Tassels

(make 4 in B, 4 in C)
For each tassel, wrap a length of yarn around the width of the card 24 times.
Cut a 20.5cm (8in) length of yarn in the same colour, thread under the wraps at one end and tie to make the hanging ring. Slide the wraps off the piece of card. Tie a 15cm (6in) length of yarn in the same colour around near the top of the tassel and knot securely. Trim the bottom ends level.

Make it yours

Change up the colours of the tassels to match the décor, or work in bright shades for a rainbow finish.

Making up and finishing

Thread the 30 wooden beads onto a length of grey T-shirt yarn.
Loop over the end and knot to create an even-sized hanging ring of approx. 13cm (5¼in) at each end of the T-shirt yarn.
Space the beads evenly along the length, leaving 13cm (5¼in) gap before the hanging rings.
Leaving one bead at the start and two beads between each accent, add a tassel in B, a star, and a tassel in C. Repeat across the length, finishing with one bead.

TIPS This garland is for decoration only. Beads can be hazardous to small children.

Ensure all the beads are fully secured and keep safely out of reach of children and babies. Using a T-shirt yarn gives the garland added strength and since it is chunky the beads are held firmly in place.

Leave the yarn ends long after finishing each of the motifs; these tails can be used to create the hanging rings.

Blocking the star motifs gives them the neat points – take time to pin them out fully for really neat stars.

Rainbow Comforter

Taking inspiration from a rainbow in both shape and colour, this unique blanket is just the right size for the stroller or using as a comforter.

SKILL RATING: ● ●

YARN AND MATERIALS

King Cole Subtle Drifter Chunky (69% acrylic, 25% cotton, 6% wool) chunky (bulky) yarn, approx. 156m (170yd) per 100g (3½oz) ball
1 ball each of:
Calico 4666 (cream) (A)
Mustard 4665 (yellow) (B)
Walnut 4668 (brown) (C)
Rose 4672 (pink) (D)
Sky 4675 (light blue) (E)
Denim 4670 (dark blue) (F)

HOOK AND EQUIPMENT

6mm (US size J/10) hook
Stitch markers (optional)
Yarn needle

FINISHED MEASUREMENTS

73.5cm (29in) wide x 81.5cm (32in) long

TENSION (GAUGE)

12 sts x 6 rows measure 10cm (4in) working treble, using 6mm (US size J/10) hook.

ABBREVIATIONS

See page 126.

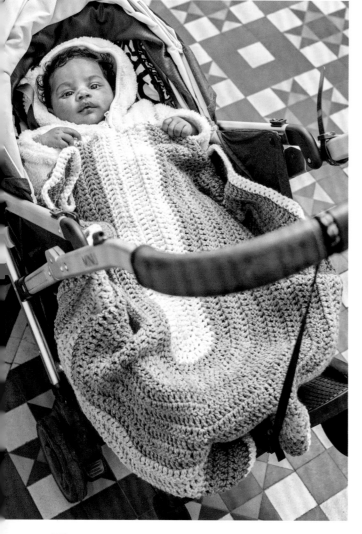

Comforter

Foundation chain: Using A, ch45.
Row 1: Beg in 4th ch from hook (missed 3-ch counts as 1tr), 1tr in next 41 ch, 6tr in last ch, rotate work and cont along second side of chain, 1tr in next 42 ch. *(90 sts)* Turn to work back in opposite direction.
Row 2: Ch3 (counts as 1tr throughout), 1tr in next 41 sts, [2tr in next st] 6 times, 1tr in last 42 sts, turn. *(96 sts)*
Row 3: Ch3, 1tr in next 41 sts, [2tr in next st, 1tr in next st] 6 times, 1tr in last 42 sts, turn. *(102 sts)*
Row 4: Change to B, ch3, 1tr in next 41 sts, [2tr in next st, 1tr in next 2 sts] 6 times, 1tr in last 42 sts, turn. *(108 sts)*

TIPS This pattern is worked back and forth in rows: the row extends down both sides of the foundation chain to form a 'U' shape. Turning the work and working back in the opposite direction after each row offsets the increases to make a neat curve that lays flat.

Locking stitch markers are useful to help keep track of stitches and placement of increases.

Make it yours

Change up the colours and work to create a traditional red, orange, yellow, green, blue rainbow.

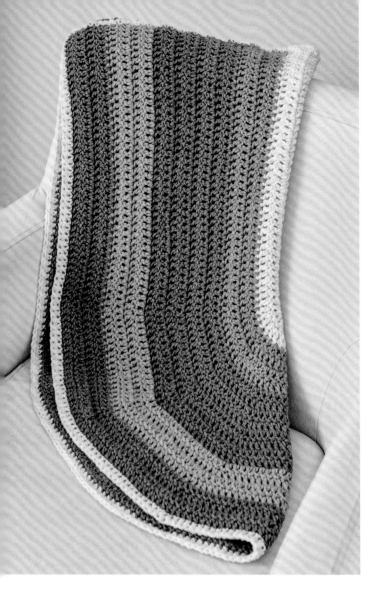

Row 15: Ch3, 1tr in next 41 sts, [2tr in next st, 1tr in next 13 sts] 6 times, 1tr in last 42 sts, turn. *(174 sts)*
Row 16: Change to E, ch3, 1tr in next 41 sts, [2tr in next st, 1tr in next 14 sts] 6 times, 1tr in last 42 sts, turn. *(180 sts)*
Row 17: Ch3, 1tr in next 41 sts, [2tr in next st, 1tr in next 15 sts] 6 times, 1tr in last 42 sts, turn. *(186 sts)*
Row 18: Ch3, 1tr in next 41 sts, [2tr in next st, 1tr in next 16 sts] 6 times, 1tr in last 42 sts, turn. *(192 sts)*
Row 19: Ch3, 1tr in next 41 sts, [2tr in next st, 1tr in next 17 sts] 6 times, 1tr in last 42 sts, turn. *(198 sts)*
Row 20: Change to F, ch3, 1tr in next 41 sts, [2tr in next st, 1tr in next 18 sts] 6 times, 1tr in last 42 sts, turn. *(204 sts)*
Row 21: Ch3, 1tr in next 41 sts, [2tr in next st, 1tr in next 19 sts] 6 times, 1tr in last 42 sts, turn. *(210 sts)*
Row 22: Ch3, 1tr in next 41 sts, [2tr in next st, 1tr in next 20 sts] 6 times, 1tr in last 42 sts, turn. *(216 sts)*
Row 23: Ch3, 1tr in next 41 sts, [2tr in next st, 1tr in next 21 sts] 6 times, 1tr in last 42 sts, turn. *(222 sts)*

BORDER

Change to A, ch3, 1tr in each st to end, do not turn, evenly work tr along straight edge of blanket at a rate of approx. 2tr per row end, join with a sl st in first st. Fasten off.

Making up and finishing

Weave in all ends and block neatly to measurements (see page 123).

Row 5: Ch3, 1tr in next 41 sts, [2tr in next st, 1tr in next 3 sts] 6 times, 1tr in last 42 sts, turn. *(114 sts)*
Row 6: Ch3, 1tr in next 41 sts, [2tr in next st, 1tr in next 4 sts] 6 times, 1tr in last 42 sts, turn. *(120 sts)*
Row 7: Ch3, 1tr in next 41 sts, [2tr in next st, 1tr in next 5 sts] 6 times, 1tr in last 42 sts, turn. *(126 sts)*
Row 8: Change to C, ch3, 1tr in next 41 sts, [2tr in next st, 1tr in next 6 sts] 6 times, 1tr in last 42 sts, turn. *(132 sts)*
Row 9: Ch3, 1tr in next 41 sts, [2tr in next st, 1tr in next 7 sts] 6 times, 1tr in last 42 sts, turn. *(138 sts)*
Row 10: Ch3, 1tr in next 41 sts, [2tr in next st, 1tr in next 8 sts] 6 times, 1tr in last 42 sts, turn. *(144 sts)*
Row 11: Ch3, 1tr in next 41 sts, [2tr in next st, 1tr in next 9 sts] 6 times, 1tr in last 42 sts, turn. *(150 sts)*
Row 12: Change to D, ch3, 1tr in next 41 sts, [2tr in next st, 1tr in next 10 sts] 6 times, 1tr in last 42 sts, turn. *(156 sts)*
Row 13: Ch3, 1tr in next 41 sts, [2tr in next st, 1tr in next 11 sts] 6 times, 1tr in last 42 sts, turn. *(162 sts)*
Row 14: Ch3, 1tr in next 41 sts, [2tr in next st, 1tr in next 12 sts] 6 times, 1tr in last 42 sts, turn. *(168 sts)*

Star Blanket

This bold star blanket is the perfect accent for a nursery or a cosy cot. The geometric shape features a repeated colour stripe pattern, making it a really stand-out design.

SKILL RATING: ● ●

YARN AND MATERIALS

Stylecraft Special Chunky (100% acrylic) DK (light worsted) weight yarn, approx. 144m (157yd) per 100g (3½oz) ball

   1 ball each of:
   Cream 1005 (A)
   Lemon 1020 (light yellow) (B)
   Saffron 1081 (light orange) (C)
   White 1001 (D)
   Spice 1711 (dark orange) (E)

HOOK AND EQUIPMENT

6mm (US size J/10) hook

Stitch markers

Yarn needle

FINISHED MEASUREMENTS

Approximate length 55cm (21¾in) from centre to tip of one point

TENSION (GAUGE)

12 sts x 6 rows measure 10cm (4in) working treble, using 6mm (US size J/10) hook.

ABBREVIATIONS

See page 126.

Make it yours

You can increase the size of the star blanket by simply following the pattern as set and continuing with the same order of yarn colours. You will need to increase the yarn quantities accordingly to accommodate a larger size.

This pattern is worked around the star, using increases and missed stitches to create the shaping.

Using stitch markers to indicate the decreases will help you to follow the pattern set in the initial rounds.

Blocking is an important finishing technique; it sets the stitches to really show off the points of the star design.

Round 5: Change to E, sl st in next st, ch3, 1tr in next 5 sts, [(3tr, ch2, 3tr) in next ch sp, 1tr in next 6 sts, miss 2 sts, 1tr in next 6 sts] 4 times, (3tr, ch2, 3tr) in next ch sp, 1tr in next 6 sts, miss 2 sts, join with a sl st in top of 3-ch. *(90 tr and 5 ch sps)*
Fasten off E.
Round 6: Change to A, sl st in next st, ch3, 1tr in next 7 sts, [(3tr, ch2, 3tr) in next ch sp, 1tr in next 8 sts, miss 2 sts, 1tr in next 8 sts] 4 times, (3tr, ch2, 3tr) in next ch sp, 1tr in next 8 sts, miss 2 sts, join with a sl st in top of 3-ch.
Cont in patt as set working following colour sequence:
Round 7: B.
Round 8: C.
Round 9: D.
Round 10: E.
Rep five-round colour sequence twice more.

BORDER
Round 1: Change to A, ch1 (does not count as a st throughout), [1dc in each st to 2-ch sp, (1dc, ch1, 1dc) in 2-ch sp] 5 times, 1dc in each st to end, join with a sl st in first st.
Round 2: Change to E, ch1, [1dc in each st to 2-ch sp, (1dc, ch1, 1dc) in 2-ch sp] 5 times, 1dc in each st to end, join with a sl st in first st.
Fasten off.

Making up and finishing
Weave in all ends and block neatly to measurements (see page 123).

Blanket
Using A, make a magic ring.
Round 1: Ch6 (counts as 1tr and ch3), [3tr into ring, ch3] 4 times, 2tr into ring, join with a sl st in 3rd ch of beg 6-ch. *(15 tr and 5 ch sps)*
Fasten off A.
Round 2: Change to B, sl st in next ch sp, ch3 (counts as 1tr throughout), (2tr, ch2, 3tr) in same ch sp, [(3tr, ch2, 3tr) in next ch sp] 4 times, join with a sl st in top of 3-ch. *(30 tr and 5 ch sps)*
Fasten off B.
Round 3: Change to C, sl st in next st, ch3, 1tr in next st, [(3tr, ch2, 3tr) in next ch sp, 1tr in next 2 sts, miss 2 sts, 1tr in next 2 sts] 4 times, (3tr, ch2, 3tr) in next ch sp, 1tr in next 2 sts, miss 2 sts, join with a sl st in top of 3-ch. *(50 tr and 5 ch sps)*
Fasten off C.
Round 4: Change to D, sl st in next st, ch3, 1tr in next 3 sts, [(3tr, ch2, 3tr) in next ch sp, 1tr in next 4 sts, miss 2 sts, 1tr in next 4 sts] 4 times, (3tr, ch2, 3tr) in next ch sp, 1tr in next 4 sts, miss 2 sts, join with a sl st to top of 3-ch. *(70 tr and 5 ch sps)*
Fasten off D.

Nesting Baskets

Whether for stowing toys and teddies or for tidying nappy change supplies, these crochet baskets are a great addition to a nursery. Worked in a chunky jersey yarn, the finished basket is robust yet soft.

SKILL RATING: ●

YARN AND MATERIALS

Wool and the Gang Jersey Be Good (upcycled T-shirt yarn, 98% cotton, 2% elastane) super chunky (super bulky) weight yarn, approx. 100m (109yd) per 500g (17½oz) ball
  1 ball each of:
  Peach Cheeks (A)
  Baby Got Back Blue (B)
  Cappuccino Cream (C)

HOOK AND EQUIPMENT

10mm (US size N–P/15) hook

Stitch marker

Extra large yarn needle

FINISHED MEASUREMENTS

Small basket: 19cm (7½in) across, 13cm (5¼in) tall

Large basket: 24cm (9½in) across, 15cm (6in) tall

TENSION (GAUGE)

7.5 sts x 8 rows measure 10cm (4in) working double crochet, using 10mm (US size N–P/15) hook.

ABBREVIATIONS

See page 126.

Make it yours

Create striped baskets by working a couple of rounds in one colour and then changing to a contrast colour.

TIPS The edge of the base is created by working through the back loop only (BLO), this is the loop that is furthest away from your body as you hold the work.

Weaving in the ends with larger yarns can be tricky; a smaller crochet hook can be used to help tuck them into the crochet fabric.

Small basket

Using A, make a magic ring.
Round 1: 6dc into ring.
Work in a continuous spiral, placing st marker at start of round.
Round 2: 2dc in each st around. *(12 sts)*
Round 3: *2dc, 1dc in next st; rep from * to end. *(18 sts)*
Round 4: *2dc, 1dc in next 2 sts; rep from * to end. *(24 sts)*
Round 5: *2dc, 1dc in next 3 sts; rep from * to end. *(30 sts)*
Round 6: *2dc, 1dc in next 4 sts; rep from * to end. *(36 sts)*
Round 7: *2dc, 1dc in next 5 sts; rep from * to end. *(42 sts)*
Round 8: 1dcBLO in each st around.
Rounds 9–16: 1dc in each st around.
Round 17: Change to C, 1dc in each st around.
Round 18: 1dc in each st around, join with a sl st in first st.
Fasten off.

Large basket

Using B, make a magic ring.
Round 1: 6dc into ring.
Work in a continuous spiral, placing st marker at start of round.
Round 2: 2dc in each st around. *(12 sts)*
Round 3: *2dc, 1dc in next st; rep from * to end. *(18 sts)*
Round 4: *2dc, 1dc in next 2 sts; rep from * to end. *(24 sts)*
Round 5: *2dc, 1dc in next 3 sts; rep from * to end. *(30 sts)*
Round 6: *2dc, 1dc in next 4 sts; rep from * to end. *(36 sts)*
Round 7: *2dc, 1dc in next 5 sts; rep from * to end. *(42 sts)*
Round 8: *2dc, 1dc in next 6 sts; rep from * to end. *(48 sts)*
Round 9: *2dc, 1dc in next 7 sts; rep from * to end. *(54 sts)*
Round 10: 1dcBLO in each st around.
Rounds 11–19: 1dc in each st around.
Round 20: Change to C, 1dc in each st around.
Round 21: 1dc in each st around, join with a sl st in first st.
Fasten off.

Making up and finishing

Weave in yarn ends neatly (see page 123) and ease baskets into shape.

Hooded Blanket

This super-sized blanket is ideal to snuggle up with. The hood makes it easy to wrap up the child, while the chunky yarn gives a calming weighted feel.

SKILL RATING: ● ●

YARN AND MATERIALS

Sirdar Hayfield Bonus Super Chunky (100% acrylic) super chunky (super bulky) weight yarn, approx. 82m (90yd) per 100g (3½oz) ball
  1 ball each of:
  Platinum 559 (grey) (A)
  Cornflour 610 (pale blue) (B)
  Lake Blue 566 (pale purple) (C)
  Ocean Blue 609 (dark blue) (D)
  Peacock 560 (turquoise) (E)

HOOK AND EQUIPMENT

10mm (US size N–P/15) hook

Large-eye yarn needle

FINISHED MEASUREMENTS

106.5cm (42in) x 117cm (46in) excluding hood

TENSION (GAUGE)

Two and a half 3-tr clusters x 4 rows measure 10cm (4in), using 10mm (US size N–P/15) hook.

ABBREVIATIONS

See page 126.

Make it yours

The size of this pattern can be adapted to make an even larger blanket – simply continue increasing each round as set, remembering to adjust the yarn quantities.

Blanket

Using A, ch13.
Round 1: 2tr in 4th ch from hook, ch1, miss next 2 ch, [3tr in next ch, ch1, miss next 2 ch] twice, (3tr, ch2, 3tr, ch2, 3tr) in last ch, rotate to work down second side, [ch1, miss next 2 ch, 3tr in next ch] twice, ch1, (3tr, ch2, 3tr) in last ch, ch2, join with a sl st in top of 3-ch. Fasten off A.

Round 2: Join B in next ch sp, ch3 (counts as 1tr throughout), 2tr in same sp, [ch1, 3tr in next ch sp] twice, ch1, (3tr, ch2, 3tr) in next corner sp, ch1, (3tr, ch2, 3tr) in next corner sp, [ch1, 3tr in next ch sp] 3 times, ch1, (3tr, ch2, 3tr) in next corner sp, ch1, (3tr, ch2, 3tr) in next corner sp, ch1, join with a sl st in top of 3-ch. Fasten off B.

Round 3: Join C in next ch sp, ch3, 2tr in same sp, ch1, *[3tr in next 1-ch sp, ch1] to corner, (3tr, ch2, 3tr) in corner 2-ch sp, ch1; rep from * three times, [3tr in next 1-ch sp, ch1] to end, join with a sl st in top of 3-ch. Fasten off C.

Round 4: Join D in next ch sp, ch3, 2tr in same sp, ch1, *[3tr in next 1-ch sp, ch1] to corner, (3tr, ch2, 3tr) in corner 2-ch sp, ch1; rep from * three times, [3tr in next 1-ch sp, ch1] to end, join with a sl st in top of 3-ch. Fasten off D.

Round 5: Join E in next ch sp, ch3, 2tr in same sp, ch1, *[3tr in next 1-ch sp, ch1] to corner, (3tr, ch2, 3tr) in corner 2-ch sp, ch1; rep from * three times, [3tr in next 1-ch sp, ch1] to end, join with a sl st in top of 3-ch. Fasten off E.

Cont in patt as set, changing colours with each round until 20 rounds have been worked in total.

BORDER

Change to A, ch1 (does not count as st), 1dc in each st and ch around, join with a sl st in first st.
Set aside to make hood.

Hood

Work as for blanket to end of Round 5.

Round 6: Join A in next ch sp, ch3, 2tr in same sp, ch1, *[3tr in next 1-ch sp, ch1] to corner, (3tr, ch2, 3tr) in corner 2-ch sp, ch1; rep from * three times, [3tr in next 1-ch sp, ch1] to end, join with a sl st in top of 3-ch. Fasten off A.

Round 7: Rejoin A in next ch sp, ch3, 2tr in same sp, ch1, *[3tr in next 1-ch sp, ch1] to corner, (3tr, ch2, 3tr) in corner 2-ch sp, ch1; rep from * three times, [3tr in next 1-ch sp, ch1] to end, join with a sl st in top of 3-ch.

Round 8: Ch1 (does not count as st), 1dc in each st and ch around, join with a sl st in first st.
Fasten off, leaving a long yarn tail.

TIPS This pattern is an adaptation of the Granny Square, but worked to create a rectangle shape. Once a few rounds have been worked it will become easier to follow the pattern.

For safety, hooded blankets should only be used for older toddlers. Don't leave children to sleep in a hooded blanket.

Making up and finishing

Fold the two shorter edges of the hood together to create the hood seam.

Using A, insert the hook from front to back through the first st, draw the yarn through, then insert the hook front to back through the corresponding stitch on the other side. Draw the yarn through, yarn round hook and draw through all loops on the hook. Repeat to the end to join with a flat seam. Fasten off.

Centre the hood on one long side of the blanket and, using E, insert the hook from front to back through the first stitch, draw the yarn through then insert hook front to back through the corresponding stitch on the other side. Draw the yarn through, yarn round hook and draw through all loops on the hook. Repeat to the end to join with a flat seam. Fasten off.

BORDER

Join E in any st and work 1dc in each st around entire edge of blanket and hood, working (1dc, ch1, 1dc) in each corner, join with a sl st in first st.
Fasten off and weave in all ends (see page 123).

Corner-to-Corner Colourblock Cushion

This bold-coloured cushion uses a corner-to-corner crochet method, building the design in blocks of stitches as you work. Pair a trio of bright shades with a neutral tone to get a strong colour pop.

SKILL RATING: ●●

YARN AND MATERIALS

Cascade 220 Superwash (100% wool) DK (light worsted) weight yarn, approx. 200m (219yd) per 100g (3½oz) ball
  1 ball each of:
  Aspen Heather 359 (grey) (A)
  Deep Sea Coral 287 (B)
  Baby Denim 897 (blue) (C)

Small amount of Faded Rose 346 (D)

30cm (12in) cushion pad

HOOK AND EQUIPMENT

4.5mm (US size 7) hook

Yarn needle

FINISHED MEASUREMENTS

30.5cm (12in)

TENSION (GAUGE)

5.5 C2C blocks x 5.5 C2C rows measure 10cm (4in), using 4.5mm (US size 7) hook.

ABBREVIATIONS

See page 126.

Cushion panel

(make 2)
Using A, ch6.
Row 1: 1tr in 4th ch from hook, 1tr in next 2 sts, turn. *(1 x 4-tr block)*
Row 2: Ch6, 1tr in 4th ch from hook, 1tr in next 2 sts (first tr block), sl st in top of ch sp of previous block, ch3, 3tr in ch sp, turn. *(2 x 4-tr blocks)*
Row 3: Ch6, 1tr in 4th ch from hook, 1tr in next 2 sts, *sl st in ch sp in next block, ch3, 3tr in same ch sp; rep from * to end, turn. *(3 x 4-tr blocks)*
Row 4: Ch6, 1tr in 4th ch from hook, 1tr in next 2 sts, *sl st in ch sp in next block, ch3, 3tr in same ch sp; rep from * to end, turn. *(4 x 4-tr blocks)*
Row 5: Ch6, 1tr in 4th ch from hook, 1tr in next 2 sts, *sl st in ch sp in next block, ch3, 3tr in same ch sp; rep from * to end, turn. *(5 x 4-tr blocks)*
Row 6: Ch6, 1tr in 4th ch from hook, 1tr in next 2 sts, *sl st in ch sp in next block, ch3, 3tr in same ch sp; rep from * to end, turn. *(6 x 4-tr blocks)*
Row 7: Ch6, 1tr in 4th ch from hook, 1tr in next 2 sts, *sl st in ch sp in next block, ch3, 3tr in same ch sp; rep from * to end, turn. *(7 x 4-tr blocks)*
Row 8: Changing colours to work 1 block in B, 6 blocks in A, 1 block in C: ch6, 1tr in 4th ch from hook, 1tr in next 2 sts, *sl st in ch sp in next block, ch3, 3tr in same ch sp; rep from * to end, turn. *(8 x 4-tr blocks)*
Row 9: Changing colours to work 2 blocks in C, 5 blocks in A, 2 blocks in B: ch6, 1tr in 4th ch from hook, 1tr in next 2 sts, *sl st in ch sp in next block, ch3, 3tr in same ch sp; rep from * to end, turn. *(9 x 4-tr blocks)*
Row 10: Changing colours to work 3 blocks in B, 4 blocks in A, 3 blocks in C: ch6, 1tr in 4th ch from hook, 1tr in next 2 sts, *sl st in ch sp in next block, ch3, 3tr in same ch sp; rep from * to end, turn. *(10 x 4-tr blocks)*

- -

Make it yours

Corner-to-corner (C2C) is a crochet technique that starts on a corner and creates blocks that increase row by row to the centre point and then are decreased in the same manner. You can make the project any size by simply working more rows before the centre and then decreasing evenly.

TIP Corner-to-corner crochet is made up of blocks of stitches. It is easy to keep track of which row you are on as Row 1 has 1 block, Row 2 has 2 blocks, Row 3 has 3 blocks, and so on up to the centre point. The decreases reduce the block in the same way.

Row 11: Changing colours to work 4 blocks in C, 3 blocks in A, 4 blocks in B: ch6, 1tr in 4th ch from hook, 1tr in next 2 sts, *sl st in ch sp in next block, ch3, 3tr in same ch sp; rep from * to end, turn. *(11 x 4-tr blocks)*

Row 12: Changing colours to work 5 blocks in B, 2 blocks in A, 5 blocks in C: ch6, 1tr in 4th ch from hook, 1tr in next 2 sts, *sl st in ch sp in next block, ch3, 3tr in same ch sp; rep from * to end, turn. *(12 x 4-tr blocks)*

Row 13: Changing colours to work 6 blocks in C, 1 block in A, 6 blocks in B: ch6, 1tr in 4th ch from hook, 1tr in next 2 sts, *sl st in ch sp in next block, ch3, 3tr in same ch sp; rep from * to end, turn. *(13 x 4-tr blocks)*

Row 14: Changing colours to work 7 blocks in B, 7 blocks in C: ch6, 1tr in 4th ch from hook, 1tr in next 2 sts, *sl st in ch sp in next block, ch3, 3tr in same ch sp; rep from * to end, turn. *(14 x 4-tr blocks)*

Row 15: Changing colours to work 7 blocks in C, 1 block in D, 7 blocks in B: ch6, 1tr in 4th ch from hook, 1tr in next 2 sts, *sl st in ch sp in next block, ch3, 3tr in same ch sp; rep from * to end, turn. *(15 x 4-tr blocks)*

Row 16: Changing colours to work 7 blocks in B, 2 blocks in D, 7 blocks in C: ch6, 1tr in 4th ch from hook, 1tr in next 2 sts, *sl st in ch sp in next block, ch3, 3tr in same ch sp; rep from * to end, turn. *(16 x 4-tr blocks)*

Row 17: Changing colours to work 6 blocks in C, 3 blocks in D, 6 blocks in B: ch6, 1tr in 4th ch from hook, 1tr in next 2 sts, *sl st in ch sp in next block, ch3, 3tr in same ch sp; rep from * to end, turn. *(17 x 4-tr blocks)*

BEGIN DECREASES

Row 18: Changing colours to work 7 blocks in B, 2 blocks in D, 7 blocks in C: sl st in 3 tr sts from previous row, sl st in ch sp, *ch3, 3tr in same ch sp, sl st in next ch sp; rep from * to end, turn. *(16 x 4-tr blocks)*

Row 19: Changing colours to work 7 blocks in C, 1 block in D, 7 blocks in B: sl st in 3 tr sts from previous row, sl st in ch sp, *ch3, 3tr in same ch sp, sl st in next ch sp; rep from * to end, turn. *(15 x 4-tr blocks)*

Row 20: Changing colours to work 7 blocks in B, 7 blocks in C: sl st in 3 tr sts from previous row, sl st in ch sp, *ch3, 3tr in same ch sp, sl st in next ch sp; rep from * to end, turn. *(14 x 4-tr blocks)*

Row 21: Changing colours to work 6 blocks in C, 1 block in A, 6 blocks in B: sl st in 3 tr sts from previous row, sl st in ch sp, *ch3, 3tr in same ch sp, sl st in next ch sp; rep from * to end, turn. *(13 x 4-tr blocks)*

Row 22: Changing colours to work 5 blocks in B, 2 blocks in A, 5 blocks in C: sl st in 3 tr sts from previous row, sl st in ch sp, *ch3, 3tr in same ch sp, sl st in next ch sp; rep from * to end, turn. *(12 x 4-tr blocks)*

Row 23: Changing colours to work 4 blocks in C, 3 blocks in A, 4 blocks in B: sl st in 3 tr sts from previous row, sl st in ch sp, *ch3, 3tr in same ch sp, sl st in next ch sp; rep from * to end, turn. *(11 x 4-tr blocks)*

Row 24: Changing colours to work 3 blocks in B, 4 blocks in A, 3 blocks in C: sl st in 3 tr sts from previous row, sl st in ch sp, *ch3, 3tr in same ch sp, sl st in next ch sp; rep from * to end, turn. *(10 x 4-tr blocks)*

Row 25: Changing colours to work 2 blocks in C, 5 blocks in A, 2 blocks in B: sl st in 3 tr sts from previous row, sl st in ch sp, *ch3, 3tr in same ch sp, sl st in next ch sp; rep from * to end, turn. *(9 x 4-tr blocks)*

Row 26: Changing colours to work 1 block in B, 6 blocks in A, 1 block in C: sl st in 3 tr sts from previous row, sl st in ch sp, *ch3, 3tr in same ch sp, sl st in next ch sp; rep from * end, turn. *(8 x 4-tr blocks)*
Fasten off other colours and cont in A only.

Row 27: Sl st in 3 tr sts from previous row, sl st in ch sp, *ch3, 3tr in same ch sp, sl st in next ch sp; rep from * to end, turn. *(7 x 4-tr blocks)*

TIP The edging is used to seal up the cushion around the cushion pad – be sure that the stitches are worked securely to prevent the seam from gaping.

Row 28: Sl st in 3 tr sts from previous row, sl st in ch sp, *ch3, 3tr in same ch sp, sl st in next ch sp; rep from * to end, turn. *(6 x 4-tr blocks)*

Row 29: Sl st in 3 tr sts from previous row, sl st in ch sp, *ch3, 3tr in same ch sp, sl st in next ch sp; rep from * to end, turn. *(5 x 4-tr blocks)*

Row 30: Sl st in 3 tr sts from previous row, sl st in ch sp, *ch3, 3tr in same ch sp, sl st in next ch sp; rep from * to end, turn. *(4 x 4-tr blocks)*

Row 31: Sl st in 3 tr sts from previous row, sl st in ch sp, *ch3, 3tr in same ch sp, sl st in next ch sp; rep from * to end, turn. *(3 x 4-tr blocks)*

Row 32: Sl st in 3 tr sts from previous row, sl st in ch sp, *ch3, 3tr in same ch sp, sl st in next ch sp; rep from * to, turn. *(2 x 4-tr blocks)*

Row 33: Sl st in 3 tr sts from previous row, sl st in ch sp, *ch3, 3tr in same ch sp, sl st in next ch sp; rep from * to end. *(1 x 4-tr block)*
Fasten off.

Making up and finishing

Weave in the yarn ends for all the colours on the WS.
Block neatly to finished measurements (see page 123).
Hold the cushion front and back with WS together.
Join in A and work along the straight edges with 1dc in each stitch, working through both the front and back to join, and working (1dc, ch1, 1dc) at each corner.
Insert cushion pad before closing up the last side.
Join with a sl st in first st and fasten off.
Weave in remaining yarn ends.

Heart Mobile

This sweet heart mobile features large and small plush hearts. These are worked quickly in the round and, because they only use a small amount of yarn, they make a great stash-buster project.

SKILL RATING: ●

YARN AND MATERIALS

Sirdar Happy Cotton (100% cotton) DK (light worsted) weight yarn, approx. 43m (47yd) per 20g (¾oz) ball

   1 ball each of:
   Bubbly 785 (turquoise) (A)
   Angel 796 (pale blue) (B)
   Juicy 792 (orange) (C)
   Sundae 787 (pale yellow) (D)
   Laundry 782 (green) (E)
   Squeaky 783 (pale green) (F)
   Bubblegum 799 (bright pink) (G)
   Piggy 764 (pink) (H)

Assortment of wooden beads

Wooden mobile frame

Child-safe toy stuffing (fiberfill)

Twine

HOOK AND EQUIPMENT

4mm (US size G/6) hook

Stitch marker

Yarn needle

FINISHED MEASUREMENTS

Large heart: 5cm (2in)

Small heart: 4cm (1½in)

TENSION (GAUGE)

Not applicable for this project, crochet to create a firm fabric.

ABBREVIATIONS

See page 126.

- -

Make it yours

Create stripes or ombre hearts by working with both the light and dark shades of each colour on a single heart.

- -

Large heart

(make 8, one in each colour)

FIRST HALF

Using any colour, make a magic ring.
Round 1: 6dc into ring. *(6 sts)*
Work in a continuous spiral, placing marker for start of round.
Round 2: 2dc in each st around. *(12 sts)*
Round 3: *1dc in next 3 sts, 2dc in next st; rep from * to end. *(15 sts)*
Round 4: 1dc in each st to end.
Fasten off.

SECOND HALF

Rep Rounds 1–4 to make second half, do not fasten off. Weave in ends from magic rings and tail on first half. Place two halves next to each other.
Round 5: With two halves together, RS facing, work 1dc in next 2 sts, working through both pieces to join them. Place marker for start of round (on first 1dc after joining sts), 1dc in each st to end. *(28 sts)*
Round 6: 1dc in each st to end.

Round 7: *1dc in next 5 sts, dc2tog; rep from * to end. *(24 sts)*

Round 8: *1dc in next 6 sts, dc2tog; rep from * to end. *(21 sts)*

Round 9: *1dc in next 5 sts, dc2tog; rep from * to end. *(18 sts)*

Begin stuffing heart.

Round 10: *1dc in next st, dc2tog; rep from * to end. *(12 sts)*

Round 11: 1dc in each st to end.

Round 12: *1dc in next 2 sts, dc2tog; rep from * to end. *(9 sts)*

Finish stuffing heart.

Round 13: *1dc in next st, dc2tog; rep from * to end. *(6 sts)*

Cut the yarn and weave through the stitches, draw up to make point of heart.

Fasten off and weave in end (see page 123).

Small heart

(make 8, one in each colour)

FIRST HALF

Using any colour, make a magic ring.

Round 1: 6dc into ring. *(6 sts)*

Work in a continuous spiral, placing marker for start of round.

Round 2: 2dc in each st around. *(12 sts)*

Rounds 3 and 4: 1dc in each st around.

Pull yarn through last st and cut.

SECOND HALF

Rep Rounds 1–4 to make second half, do not fasten off. Weave in ends from magic rings and tail on first half. Place two halves next to each other.

Round 5: With two halves together, RS facing, work 1dc in next 2 sts, working through both pieces to join them. Place marker for start of round (on first 1dc after joining sts), 1dc in each st to end. *(22 sts)*

Round 6: 1dc in each st to end.

Round 7: *1dc in next 3 sts, dc2tog; rep from * to last 2 sts, 1dc in last 2 sts. *(18 sts)*

Round 8: *1dc in next 4 sts, dc2tog; rep from * to end. *(15 sts)*

Round 9: *1dc in next 3 sts, dc2tog; rep from * to end. *(12 sts)*

Begin stuffing heart.

Round 10: *1dc in next 2 sts, dc2tog; rep from * to end. *(9 sts)*

Finish stuffing heart.

Round 11: *1dc in next st, dc2tog; rep from * to end. *(6 sts)*

Cut the yarn and weave through the stitches, draw up to make point of heart.

Fasten off and weave in end (see page 123).

Making up and finishing

Using a yarn needle, thread a matching pair of hearts onto a length of twine, with the large heart at the bottom and the small heart at the top. Space evenly and knot into place. Secure through the mobile frame and knot into place, adding a wooden bead at the base of the large heart as desired. Repeat to hang all the hearts to the frame. Add a hanging loop of twine to finish.

TIPS Weave in the ends from the magic ring before working the decreases because the space inside the heart is very small.

This mobile is a decorative piece and not a toy. When securing the elements together be sure to make the knots secure to prevent any hazard to babies and young children.

Dreamy Llama Wall Hanging

Brighten up baby's bedroom with a colourful wall hanging. This character design is worked in simple double crochet and different colours to make a picture in yarn, accented with tassels and flowers.

SKILL RATING: ●

YARN AND MATERIALS

Sirdar Snuggly DK (55% nylon, 45% acrylic) DK (light worsted) weight yarn, approx. 165m (179yd) per 50g (1¾oz) ball
  1 ball each of:
  Sky 216 (blue) (A)
  Cream 303 (B)
  Sorbet 509 (pale orange) (C)
  Spicy Pink 350 (bright pink) (D)
  Aqua 490 (green) (E)

Small amount of grey DK (light worsted) yarn for face details

30cm (12in) wooden dowel

Twine for hanging

HOOK AND EQUIPMENT

4mm (US size G/6) hook

Yarn needle

FINISHED MEASUREMENTS

23 x 29cm (9 x 11½in)

TENSION (GAUGE)

18 sts x 20 rows measure 10cm (4in) working double crochet, using 4mm (US size G/6) hook.

ABBREVIATIONS

See page 126.

- - - - - - - - - - - - - - - - - - - -

Make it yours

Once you've mastered the Dreamy Llama you can use the same size crochet canvas – 40 sts by 50 rows – to create your own fun animal designs.

- - - - - - - - - - - - - - - - - - - -

TIPS When embroidering the face details, use the crochet stitches as a guide for getting the design even and central to the character's face.

As this design is created by changing from one colour to another you can carry the non-working yarn across the back of the work. Use the working yarn to catch these 'floats' every few stitches to gently hold them to the back of the work.

Ears

(make 2)
Using B, ch5.
Row 1: 1dc in 2nd ch from hook and each ch to end, turn. *(4 sts)*
Row 2: Ch1 (does not count as a st throughout), 2dc in first st, 1dc in next 2 sts, 2dc in last st, turn. *(6 sts)*
Rows 3–6: Ch1, 1dc in each st to end, turn.
Row 7: Ch1, dc2tog, 1dc in next 2 sts, dc2tog, turn. *(4 sts)*
Row 8: Ch1, 1dc in each st to end, turn.
Row 9: Ch1, [dc2tog] twice. *(2 sts)*
Fasten off.

Flowers

(make 2 each in C and D, 1 in E)
Make a magic ring.
Round 1: 5dc into ring, join with a sl st in first st. *(5 sts)*
Round 2: Ch2 (does not count as a st), (1htr, 3tr, 1htr) in first st, *sl st in next st, (1htr, 3tr, 1htr) in same st; rep from * 3 more times to make 5 petals in total, join with a sl st in base of first st.
Fasten off.

Making up and finishing

Fold the hanging tabs over to the WS of the wall hanging and stitch into place to form loops.
Place the ears into position on top of the animal shape and sew into place. Embroider the face details (see page 125). Position the flowers in place and sew securely.
Cut 10cm (4in) lengths of yarns C, D and E. Fold five strands of one colour in half, thread the loop through a bottom stitch of the wall hanging then pull the ends through the loop to make a knotted tassle using a lark's head knot. Repeat to space seven tassels evenly along the bottom edge.
Insert the dowel into the hanging tabs and attach twine for hanging.

Wall Hanging

Using A, ch41.
Row 1: 1dc in second ch from hook and each ch to end, turn. *(40 sts)*
Rows 2–10: Ch1 (does not count as a st throughout), 10dc in A, 20dc in B, 10dc in A, turn.
Rows 11–15: Ch1, 11dc in A, 18dc in B, 11dc in A, turn.
Rows 16–18: Ch1, 13dc in A, 14dc in B, 13dc in A, turn.
Rows 19–21: Ch1, 14dc in A, 12dc in B, 14dc in A, turn.
Row 22: Ch1, 13dc in A, 14dc in B, 13dc in A, turn.
Row 23: Ch1, 12dc in A, 16dc in B, 12dc in A, turn.
Row 24: Ch1, 11dc in A, 18dc in B, 11dc in A, turn.
Row 25: Ch1, 10dc in A, 20dc in B, 10dc in A, turn.
Rows 26 and 27: Ch1, 9dc in A, 22dc in B, 9dc in A, turn.
Rows 28–32: Ch1, 8dc in A, 24dc in B, 8dc in A, turn.
Row 33: Ch1, 9dc in A, 22dc in B, 9dc in A, turn.
Rows 34 and 35: Ch1, 10dc in A, 20dc in B, 10dc in A, turn.
Row 36: Ch1, 11dc in A, 18dc in B, 11dc in A, turn.
Row 37: Ch1, 12dc in A, 16dc in B, 12dc in A, turn.
Row 38: Ch1, 13dc in A, 14dc in B, 13dc in A, turn.
Row 39: Ch1, 14dc in A, 12dc in B, 14dc in A, turn.
Row 40: Ch1, 16dc in A, 8dc in B, 16dc in A, turn.
Fasten off B.
Rows 41–50: Cont in A only, ch1, 1dc in each st to end.
Fasten off A.

HANGING TABS

With RS facing, rejoin A to upper right-hand side of wall hanging, ch1, 6dc, turn.
Work 10 rows in dc as set.
Fasten off.
Rep to add second tab to upper left-hand side and over middle 6 sts.

Mini Blanket

This small blanket is the ideal size for putting on the stroller or a pram. The cluster stitch pattern isn't just pretty: it creates a wonderfully dense fabric that gives the blanket substance and makes it a super-cosy choice.

SKILL RATING: ●●

YARN AND MATERIALS

Caron Simply Soft (100% acrylic) aran (worsted) weight yarn, approx. 288m (315yd) per 170g (6oz) ball
 1 ball each of:
 Off White 9702 (A)
 Persimmon 9754 (apricot) (B)
 Light Country Blue 9709 (C)
 Robin's Egg 9780 (pale turquoise) (D)

HOOK AND EQUIPMENT

5mm (US size H/8) hook

Yarn needle

FINISHED MEASUREMENTS

71cm (28in) square

TENSION (GAUGE)

8 cluster sts x 11 rows measure 10cm (4in), working cluster pattern using 5mm (US size H/8) hook.

ABBREVIATIONS

See page 126.

Make it yours

The colour repeats are created by using the cream yarn to break up the sequence – change this to a brighter colour for more contrast.

SPECIAL ABBREVIATION

TRC (treble cluster): yarn round hook, insert hook in st, yarn round hook and pull through a loop (3 loops on hook), yarn round hook and pull through 2 loops on hook (2 loops on hook), yarn round hook, insert hook in same st, yarn round hook and pull through a loop, yarn round hook and pull through 2 loops on hook (3 loops on hook), yarn round hook, insert hook in same st, yarn round hook and pull through a loop, yarn round hook and pull through 2 loops on hook (4 loops on hook), yarn round hook, insert hook in same st, yarn round hook and pull through a loop, yarn round hook and pull through 2 loops on hook (5 loops on hook), yarn round hook and pull through all loops on hook, ch1 to secure cluster.

Mini Blanket

Using A, ch106.
Row 1: 1dc in 2nd ch from hook and next ch, *ch1, miss 1 ch, 1dc in next ch; rep from * to last 3 ch, ch1, miss 1 ch, 1dc in each of last 2 ch, turn.
Row 2: Change to B, ch4 (counts as 1tr and 1ch throughout), TRC in each 1-ch sp to end, miss 1 dc, 1tr in last st, turn. *(51 TRC)*
Row 3: Change to A, ch1 (does not count as a st throughout), 1dc in top of tr, 1dc in ch sp before first TRC, *ch1, 1dc in next ch sp between TRC; rep from * to end working 1dc in ch sp after last TRC and 1dc in third of 4-ch, turn. *(54 dc)*
Row 4: Change to C, ch4, TRC in each 1-ch sp to end, miss 1 dc, 1tr in last st, turn. *(51 TRC)*
Row 5: Change to A, ch1, 1dc in top of tr, 1dc in ch sp before first TRC, *ch1, 1dc in next ch sp between TRC; rep from * to end working 1dc in ch sp after last TRC and 1dc in third of 4-ch, turn. *(54 dc)*
Row 6: Change to D, ch4, TRC in each 1-ch sp to end, miss 1 dc, 1tr in last st, turn. *(51 TRC)*
Row 7: Change to A, ch1, 1dc in top of tr, 1dc in ch sp before first TRC, *ch1, 1dc in next ch sp between TRC; rep from * to end working 1dc in ch sp after last TRC and 1dc in third of 4-ch, turn. *(54 dc)*
Rep Rows 2–7 ten more times to create 11 colour pattern repeats. Do not turn at end of final row, rotate work and continue down side of blanket, work dc evenly along edge at a rate of approx. 3 sts per 2 rows, rotate work, 1dc in each st along foundation chain, rotate work, work dc evenly along second side of blanket, join with a sl st in first st.
Fasten off.

TIPS Changing colours of yarn every row means that there are lots of ends to weave in; sew them in as you go to make the finishing process easier.

The cluster stitch is a variation of treble stitch with the last part of the stitch used to create the cluster. The pattern is a two-row repeat, so once a few rows have been worked it is an easy pattern to follow.

BORDER

Join in A at any corner, ch3 (counts as 1 tr), *1tr in each st to corner, (2tr, ch1, 2tr) in corner st; rep from * to end, join with a sl st in first st.
Fasten off.

Making up and finishing

Weave in ends and block neatly to finished measurements (see page 123).

Toadstool Cushion

Bring some fairy tale charm to your little one's decor with a woodland style toadstool cushion. This plush cushion is great to snuggle up with for reading time.

SKILL RATING: ●

YARN AND MATERIALS

Caron Simply Soft (100% acrylic) aran (worsted) weight yarn, approx. 288m (315yd) per 170g (6oz) ball
  1 ball each of:
  Bone 9703 (dark cream) (A)
  Fuchsia 9764 (dark pink) (B)
  Off White 9702 (C)

Light wadding such as Thermolam (optional)

Child-safe toy stuffing (fibrefill)

HOOK AND EQUIPMENT

5mm (US size H/8) hook

Stitch marker

Yarn needle

FINISHED MEASUREMENTS

38 x 46cm (15 x 18in)

TENSION (GAUGE)

14 sts x 10 rows measure 10cm (4in) working half treble, using 5mm (US size H/8) hook.

ABBREVIATIONS

See page 126.

Stalk

(make 2)
Using A, ch22.
Row 1: 1htr in third ch from hook and each ch to end, turn. *(20 sts)*
Rows 2–15: Ch2 (does not count as a st), 1htr in each st to end, turn.
Fasten off.

Toadstool cap

(make 2)
Using B, ch42.
Row 1: 1htr in 3rd ch from hook and each ch to end, turn. *(40 sts)*
Row 2: Ch2 (does not count as a st throughout), 2htr in first st, 1htr in each st to last st, 2htr in last st, turn. *(42 sts)*
Row 3: Ch2, 2htr in first st, 1htr in each st to last st, 2htr in last st, turn. *(44 sts)*

Row 4: Ch2, 2htr in first st, 1htr in each st to last st, 2htr in last st, turn. *(46 sts)*
Row 5: Ch2, 1htr in each st to end, turn.
Row 6: Ch2, 2htr in first st, 1htr in each st to last st, 2htr in last st, turn. *(48 sts)*
Row 7: Ch2, 1htr in each st to end, turn.
Row 8: Ch2, 2htr in first st, 1htr in each st to last st, 2htr in last st, turn. *(50 sts)*
Rows 9 and 10: Ch2, 1htr in each st to end, turn.
Row 11: Ch2, htr2tog, 1htr in each st to last 2 sts, htr2tog, turn. *(48 sts)*
Row 12: Ch2, htr2tog, 1htr in each st to last 2 sts, htr2tog, turn. *(46 sts)*
Row 13: Ch2, 1htr in each st to end, turn.
Row 14: Ch2, [htr2tog] twice, 1htr in each st to last 2 sts, htr2tog, turn. *(43 sts)*
Row 15: Ch2, 1htr in each st to end, turn.
Row 16: Ch2, [htr2tog] twice, 1htr in each st to last 2 sts, htr2tog, turn. *(40 sts)*
Row 17: Ch2, 1htr in each st to end, turn.
Row 18: Ch2, [htr2tog] twice, 1htr in each st to last 2 sts, htr2tog, turn. *(37 sts)*
Row 19: Ch2, htr2tog, 1htr in each st to last 4 sts, [htr2tog] twice, turn. *(34 sts)*
Row 20: Ch2, [htr2tog] twice, 1htr in each st to last 2 sts, htr2tog, turn. *(31 sts)*
Row 21: Ch2, htr2tog, 1htr in each st to last 4 sts, [htr2tog] twice, turn. *(28 sts)*

TIPS When sewing the white accents onto the surface of the toadstool, move them around to create your preferred placement and safety pin in place until you sew them securely.

Trimming a piece of light wadding (Thermolam) and placing in the inside of the cushion against the wrong side of the crochet fabric is a great way to help keep the stuffing inside the stitches.

Make it yours

For a magical woodland theme, work a few toadstool cushions and vary the shades of yarn used for the toadstool cap for a more natural finish.

Work in a continuous spiral, placing marker for start of round.
Round 2: 2dc in each st to end. *(12 sts)*

MEDIUM AND LARGE ONLY
Round 3: *1dc in next st, 2dc in next st; rep from * to end. *(18 sts)*
Round 4: *1dc in next 2 sts, 2dc in next st; rep from * to end. *(24 sts)*

LARGE ONLY
Round 5: *1dc in next 3 sts, 2dc in next st; rep from * to end. *(30 sts)*
Fasten off.

Half circle

Worked in rows back and forth.
Using C, make a magic ring.
Row 1: 6dc into ring, turn. *(6 sts)*
Row 2: Ch1 (does not count as a st throughout), *1dc in next st, 2dc in next st; rep from * to end, turn. *(9 sts)*
Row 3: Ch1, *1dc in next 2 sts, 2dc in next st; rep from * to end, turn. *(12 sts)*
Row 4: Ch1, *1dc in next 3 sts, 2dc in next st; rep from * to end, turn. *(15 sts)*
Row 5: Ch1, *1dc in next 4 sts, 2dc in next st; rep from * to end, turn. *(18 sts)*
Row 6: Ch1, *1dc in next 5 sts, 2dc in next st; rep from * to end, turn. *(21 sts)*
Row 7: Ch1, *1dc in next 6 sts, 2dc in next st; rep from * to end, turn. *(24 sts)*
Row 8: Ch1, *1dc in next 7 sts, 2dc in next st; rep from * to end. *(27 sts)*
Fasten off.

Making up and finishing

Block all pieces (see page 123). Draw roughly around all stalk and cap pieces onto light wadding (Thermolam) and cut out.
Hold two stalk pieces with WS together and join with a slip stitch around three edges. Slide in the light wadding pieces and stuff inside. Repeat to seam and stuff the toadstool cap. Join stalk and toadstool cap together, adding more stuffing as needed.
Arrange the circles onto the surface of the cap and sew on securely.
Weave in all ends (see page 123).

Row 22: Ch2, [htr2tog] twice, 1htr in each st to last 2 sts, htr2tog, turn. *(25 sts)*
Row 23: Ch2, htr2tog, 1htr in each st to last 4 sts, [htr2tog] twice, turn. *(22 sts)*
Row 24: Ch2, [htr2tog] twice, 1htr in each st to last 2 sts, htr2tog, turn. *(19 sts)*
Row 25: Ch2, htr2tog, 1htr in each st to last 4 sts, [htr2tog] twice, turn. *(16 sts)*
Row 26: Ch2, [htr2tog] twice, 1htr in each st to last 2 sts, htr2tog, turn. *(13 sts)*
Row 27: Ch2, htr2tog, 1htr in each st to last 4 sts, [htr2tog] twice, turn. *(10 sts)*
Row 28: Ch2, htr2tog, 1htr in each st to last 2 sts, htr2tog, turn. *(8 sts)*
Row 29: Ch2, 1htr in each st to end, turn.
Row 30: Ch2, htr2tog, 1htr in each st to last 2 sts, htr2tog, turn. *(6 sts)*
Row 31: Ch2, 1htr in each st to end, turn.
Row 32: Ch2, htr2tog, 1htr in each st to last 2 sts, htr2tog, turn. *(4 sts)*
Row 33: Ch2, htr2tog, 1htr in each st to end. *(3 sts)*
Fasten off.

Circles

(make 2 small, 2 medium, 2 large)
Using C, make a magic ring.
Round 1: 6dc into ring. *(6 sts)*

Bold Granny Square Blanket

The classic granny square is always a crowd pleaser. This design is worked in the boldest of rainbow shades to give it a striking, modern feel.

SKILL RATING: ● ●

YARN AND MATERIALS

Stylecraft Special DK (100% acrylic) DK (light worsted) weight yarn, approx. 295m (323yd) per 100g (3½oz) ball
  1 ball each of:
  Lipstick 1246 (red) (A)
  Clementine 1853 (orange) (B)
  Citron 1263 (yellow) (C)
  Apple 1852 (green) (D)
  Aster 1003 (blue) (E)
  Proper Purple 1855 (dark purple) (F)
  Magenta 1084 (violet-pink) (G)
2 balls of Cream 1005 (H)

HOOK AND EQUIPMENT

4mm (US size G/6) hook

Yarn needle

FINISHED MEASUREMENTS

89 x 114.5cm (35 x 45in)

TENSION (GAUGE)

Each 4-round granny square measures 9.5cm (3¾in) after blocking, using 4mm (US size G/6) hook.

ABBREVIATIONS

See page 126.

. . . .

Make it yours

The colours for this blanket are set out in rainbow order, but you can create your own colourful design by alternating the shades across each of the rows, or creating another repeated pattern.

. . . .

Granny squares

(make 10 in each of A, B, C, D, E, F and G)
Make a magic ring.
Round 1: Ch3 (counts as 1tr throughout), 2tr into ring, *ch2, 3tr into ring; rep from * twice more, ch2, join with a sl st in top of 3-ch. *(4 x 3-tr blocks)*
Round 2: Sl st in next 2 sts, sl st in next ch sp, ch3, (2tr, ch2, 3tr) in same ch sp, ch1, *(3tr, ch2, 3tr) in next ch sp, ch1; rep from * twice more, join with a sl st in top of 3-ch. *(8 x 3-tr blocks)*
Round 3: Sl st in next 2 sts, sl st in next ch sp, ch3, (2tr, ch2, 3tr) in same ch sp, ch1, *3tr in next ch sp, ch1, (3tr, ch2, 3tr) in next ch sp, ch1; rep from * twice more, 3tr in next ch sp, ch1, join with a sl st in top of 3-ch. *(12 x 3-tr blocks)*
Round 4: Sl st in next 2 sts, sl st in next ch sp, ch3, (2tr, ch2, 3tr) in same ch sp, ch1, *[(3tr in next ch sp, ch1] twice, (3tr, ch2, 3tr) in next ch sp, ch1; rep from * twice more, [(3tr in next ch sp, ch1] twice, join with a sl st in top of 3-ch. *(16 x 3-tr blocks)*
Fasten off, weave in all ends and block to size.

Joining squares

Arrange the squares in 10 rows of 7 blocks.
Starting with square at upper corner of blanket, join H in corner ch sp.
Round 5: Ch3, (2tr, ch2, 3tr) in same ch sp, *[ch1, 3tr in next ch sp] 3 times, ch1, (3tr, ch2, 3tr) in corner ch sp; rep from * twice more, [ch1, 3tr in next ch sp] 3 times, ch1, join with a sl st in top of 3-ch. *(20 x 3-tr blocks)*

JOIN AS YOU GO

Once one square is complete, next square can be joined on final round at each corner ch sp and every ch sp along sides by passing loop of ch on current square through corresponding ch sp of joining square, before cont with next st (see page 124).
Cont in this manner, adding on each new square as Round 5 is worked.

BORDER

Round 1: Join H in any 1-ch sp, ch3 (counts as 1tr throughout), 2tr in same sp, *3tr in each ch sp to corner, (3tr, ch2, 3tr) in corner; rep from * 3 more times, 3tr in each ch sp to end, join with a sl st in top of 3-ch.
Round 2: Sl st in next 2 sts, sl st in next sp between 3-tr blocks, ch3, (1tr, ch2, 2tr) in same sp, (2tr, ch2, 2tr) in each sp between 3-tr blocks to corner, (2tr, ch2, 2tr, ch2, 2tr) in corner ch sp; rep from * three more times, (2tr, ch2, 2tr) in each sp between 3-tr blocks to end, join with a sl st in top of 3-ch.
Fasten off.

Making up and finishing

Weave in any remaining ends (see page 123).

TIPS Blocking is the process of pinning out a crochet piece to ease it into the correct shape. Blocking the individual granny squares makes the seaming together of this project much easier and also gives a professional finish. You can either pin out on a bed or ironing board, or you can use a purpose-made blocking board to shape the pieces (see page 123).

Although this is a large project it needn't be intimidating. Each of the 70 squares is worked up in the exact same way, making this ideal to work on in bite-sized chunks or as an on-the-go project that can easily fit into your bag.

chapter 3

Toys

Dummy Clip

Stop pacifiers or favourite toys from being dropped out of reach with a pretty dummy clip. Worked with small amounts of colourful yarn for the bobbles, this is a fantastic stash-busting project.

SKILL RATING: ●

YARN AND MATERIALS

Sirdar Happy Cotton (100% cotton) DK (light worsted) weight yarn, approx. 43m (47yd) per 20g (¾oz) ball
  1 ball each of:
  Dolly 761 (white) (A)
  Frilly 766 (lilac) (B)
  Flamingo 760 (pale pink) (C)
  Unicorn 769 (dark pink) (D)
  Angel 796 (pale blue) (E)
  Tea Time 751 (blue) (F)
  Splash 767 (turquoise) (G)
  Beach Hut 750 (dark blue) (H)

Wooden dummy clip

HOOK AND EQUIPMENT

4mm (US size G/6) hook

Yarn needle

FINISHED MEASUREMENTS

Band 20cm (7¾in) long excluding clip, 2cm (¾in) wide

TENSION (GAUGE)

Not applicable for this project.

ABBREVIATIONS

See page 126.

SPECIAL ABBREVIATION

BS (bobble stitch): using contrast yarn, *yarn round hook, insert hook in stitch, yarn round hook and pull through a loop (3 loops on hook), yarn round hook and pull through 2 loops (2 loops on hook); rep from * 4 more times in same stitch (6 loops on hook), yarn round hook, pull through all loops.

Make it yours

To create a longer band with more bobbles work a longer foundation chain, working three more chain stitches for each additional bobble.

Band

Using A, ch26.
Row 1: 1dc in 2nd ch from hook, 1dc in each ch to end, turn. *(25 sts)*
Row 2: Ch2 (counts as 1htr), 1htr in next 2 sts, drop A and join in B, BS using B in next st, drop B and pick up A, ch1 in A to close bobble, 1htr in next 2 sts, drop A and join in C, BS using C in next st, drop C and pick up A, ch1 in A to close bobble, 1htr in next 2 sts, drop A and join in D, BS using D in next st, drop D and pick up A, ch1 in A to close bobble, 1htr in next 2 sts, drop A and join in E, BS using E in next st, drop E and pick up A, ch1 in A to close bobble, 1htr in next 2 sts, drop A and join in F, BS using F in next st, drop F and pick up A, ch1 in A to close bobble, 1htr in next 2 sts, drop A and join in G, BS using G in next st, drop G and pick up A, ch1 in A to close bobble, 1htr in next 2 sts, drop A and join in H, BS using H in next st, drop H and pick up A, ch1 in A to close bobble, 1htr in next 3 sts.

BORDER

Don't turn work, cont in A only.
Work 4dc along short edge, then 1sl st in each st of long edge. At next short edge, work 2dc to halfway along short edge, ch20, sl st back in first ch (to make hanging loop), work 2dc to end of short edge, 1dc in each st along second long edge, join with a sl st in first st.
Row 1: Ch1 (does not count as a st throughout), 1dc in next 4 sts, turn. *(4 sts)*
Row 2: Ch1, 1dc in next 4 sts.
Fasten off, leaving enough yarn to sew onto dummy clip.

Making up and finishing

Fold short edge (without hanging loop) through dummy clip, and use the yarn tail to sew the crochet to it securely.
Attach the dummy to the hanging loop with a lark's head knot.
Weave in and trim ends to neaten (see page 123).

TIPS Weaving in the ends isn't easy on such small work; try knotting the threads securely and trimming short to the back of the work.

Be sure that small children are supervised when using a dummy clip to avoid hazards.

Tassel Teether

With bouncy spiral tassels this teether is a great sensory toy for small babies. Worked in bright colours, it will really stand out in the toy box.

SKILL RATING: ●

YARN AND MATERIALS

Sirdar Happy Cotton (100% cotton) DK (light worsted) weight yarn, approx. 43m (47yd) per 20g (¾oz) ball
   1 ball each of:
   Bubblegum 799 (pink) (A)
   Freckle 753 (orange) (B)
   Buttercup 771 (yellow) (C)
   Bunting 797 (blue) (D)
   Moonbeam 757 (grey) (E)

Wooden ring, 7cm (2¾in)

HOOK AND EQUIPMENT

4mm (US size G/6) hook

Yarn needle

FINISHED MEASUREMENTS

Ring 7cm (2¾in)

Each tassel 7.5cm (3in)

TENSION (GAUGE)

Not applicable for this project.

ABBREVIATIONS

See page 126.

Tassel

(make 4)
Using A, ch24.
Work 4dc in second ch from hook and in each st to end.
Fasten off, leaving a long tail to secure to teether.
Rep to make tassels in B, C and D.

Teether band

Using E, ch7.
Row 1: 1dc in 2nd ch from hook, 1dc in each ch to end, turn. *(6 sts)*
Row 2: Ch1 (does not count as a st), 1dc in each st to end, turn.
Rep Row 2 until work measures 10cm (4in) or long enough to cover half of ring.
Fasten off, leaving enough yarn to seam along length.

Making up and finishing

Sew the tassels evenly in the centre portion of the teether band using the yarn tails. Be sure to sew tightly and weave in ends (see page 123).
Place the embellished band around the wooden ring and align the long edges. Use the yarn tail to secure around the wooden ring of the teether.

Make it yours

The length of the tassels can be increased by making the initial chain longer, or you can make each tassel chunkier by working treble stitches in place of the double crochet.

TIPS Repeatedly working multiple stitches into the same stitch on the foundation chain creates a twist – the more stitches worked, the tighter the twist. Once the length has been worked, ease the strip to keep the twists running in the same direction.

Be sure to sew all the components together securely to make sure they are safe for children.

Ring Rattle

This crochet ring is the perfect size and, because it is filled with soft toy stuffing, it is ideal for baby's little hands. The two wooden rings give the toy a simple sensory finish.

Make it yours

Create chunky stripes by working more rows in each colour before changing shade – or add in more colours from your stash for a bolder design.

SKILL RATING: ●

YARN AND MATERIALS

Sirdar Happy Cotton (100% cotton) DK (light worsted) weight yarn, approx. 43m (47yd) per 20g (¾oz) ball
1 ball each of:
- Frilly 766 (lilac) (A)
- Sorbet 793 (apricot) (B)
- Sundae 787 (yellow) (C)
- Squeaky 783 (green) (D)
- Bath Time 765 (blue) (E)
- Unicorn 769 (pink) (F)

Child-safe toy stuffing (fibrefill)

Jingle bell (optional)

2 wooden rings, 5.5cm (2¼in)

HOOK AND EQUIPMENT

4mm (US size G/6) hook

Stitch marker (optional)

Yarn needle

FINISHED MEASUREMENTS

12.5cm (5in) across

TENSION (GAUGE)

20 sts x 16 rows measure 10cm (4in) working double crochet, using 4mm (US size G/6) hook.

ABBREVIATIONS

See page 126.

Rattle

Using A, ch15, sl st in first ch to join into a ring.
Round 1: Ch1 (does not count as a st throughout),
1dc in each st to end, sl sl in first st to join. *(15 sts)*
Place marker for start of round.
Round 2: Ch1, 1dc in each st to end, join with a sl st in first st.
Round 3: Change to B, ch1, 1dc in each st to end, join with a sl st in first st.
Round 4: Ch1, 1dc in each st to end, join with a sl st in first st.
Round 5: Change to C, ch1, 1dc in each st to end, join with a sl st in first st.
Round 6: Ch1, 1dc in each st to end, join with a sl st in first st.
Round 7: Change to D, ch1, 1dc in each st to end, join with a sl st in first st.
Round 8: Ch1, 1dc in each st to end, join with a sl st in first st.
Round 9: Change to E, ch1, 1dc in each st to end, join with a sl st in first st.
Round 10: Ch1, 1dc in each st to end, join with a sl st in first st.
Round 11: Change to F, ch1, 1dc in each st to end, join with a sl st in first st.

TIPS This rattle is worked as a crochet tube, so weaving the ends in when finished is practically impossible. As you work, secure the ends at each colour change and catch the yarn tails for a few stitches to secure to the inside of the tube before trimming.

The rattle needs to be stuffed fairly firmly; try adding small amounts of filling as you work to get an even padded finish.

Round 12: Ch1, 1dc in each st to end, join with a sl st in first st.
Rep Rounds 1–12 until work measures 30.5cm (12in), stuffing the tube firmly as you work and adding in a small jingle bell or two if desired.
Fasten off.

Making up and finishing

Slide the two wooden rings onto the tube. Bring the ends of the tube together to form a ring and stitch closed.

Play Balls

These crochet balls are brilliant for play time in the nursery; they are soft enough for young children and the bright colours are fun for babies, too.

SKILL RATING: ● ●

YARN AND MATERIALS

Sirdar Happy Cotton (100% cotton) DK (light worsted) weight yarn, approx. 43m (47yd) per 20g (¾oz) ball
  1 ball each of:
  Bunting 797 (blue) (A)
  Freckle 753 (orange) (A)
  Seaside 784 (turquoise) (A)
  Dolly 761 (white) (B)

Child-safe toy stuffing (fibrefill)

HOOK AND EQUIPMENT

4mm (US size G/6) hook

Stitch markers (optional)

FINISHED MEASUREMENTS

22cm (8¾in) circumference

TENSION (GAUGE)

22 sts x 24 rows measure 10cm (4in) working double crochet, using 4mm (US size G/6) hook.

ABBREVIATIONS

See page 126.

Play ball

UPPER PORTION

Using any A, make a magic ring.
Round 1: Ch1 (does not count as a st throughout), 6dc into ring, join with a sl st in first st. *(6 sts)*
Round 2: Ch1, 2dc in each st around, join with a sl st in first st. *(12 sts)*
Round 3: Ch1, *1dc, 2dc in next st; rep from * to end, join with a sl st in first st. *(18 sts)*
Round 4: Using B, ch1, *1dc in next 2 sts, 2dc in next st; rep from * to end, join with a sl st in first st. *(24 sts)*
Round 5: Ch1, *1dc in next 3 sts, 2dc in next st; rep from * to end, join with a sl st in first st. *(30 sts)*
Round 6: Ch1, *1dc in next 4 sts, 2dc in next st; rep from * to end, join with a sl st in first st. *(36 sts)*
Round 7: Change to A, ch1, *1dc in next 5 sts, 2dc in next st; rep from * to end, join with a sl st in first st. *(42 sts)*

TIPS The increase sequence set in the initial part of the design to create the lower part of the ball, is repeated as a decrease pattern to make the upper part of the ball identical.

For older children you can opt to add in dried beans, or plastic stuffing pellets in place of toy stuffing; this gives the balls a denser, heavier feeling.

CENTRE PORTION

Round 8: Ch1, 1dc in each st around, join with a sl st in first st.
Round 9: Ch1, 1dc in each st around, join with a sl st in first st.
Round 10: Change to B, ch1, 1dc in each st around, join with a sl st in first st.
Round 11: Ch1, 1dc in each st around, join with a sl st in first st.
Round 12: Ch1, 1dc in each st around, join with a sl st in first st.
Round 13: Change to A, ch1, 1dc in each st around, join with a sl st in first st.
Round 14: Ch1, 1dc in each st around, join with a sl st in first st.
Round 15: Ch1, 1dc in each st around, join with a sl st in first st.

LOWER PORTION

Round 16: Change to B, ch1, *1dc in next 5 sts, dc2tog; rep from * to end, join with a sl st in first st. *(36 sts)*
Round 17: Ch1, *1dc in next 4 sts, dc2tog; rep from * to end, join with a sl st in first st. *(30 sts)*
Round 18: Ch1, *1dc in next 3 sts, dc2tog; rep from * to end, join with a sl st in first st. *(24 sts)*
Weave in any ends from previous colour changes and stuff 80 per cent full with toy stuffing.

Make it yours

The striped design of these balls is great for playing with your own fave colour combinations – or why not make your own pattern, selecting variegated yarns or an ombre palette.

Round 19: Change to A, ch1, *1dc in next 2 sts, dc2tog; rep from * to end, join with a sl st in first st. *(18 sts)*
Round 20: Ch1, *1dc in next st, dc2tog; rep from * to end, join with a sl st in first st. *(12 sts)*
Finish stuffing.
Round 21: Dc2tog around. *(6 sts)*

Making up and finishing

Cut the yarn and weave through the stitches, draw up to close the hole and fasten off.

Fox Lovie

Part teddy, part comfort blanket, a lovie is the best of both worlds. This sweet fox character is crocheted in the softest chenille yarn for a truly plush finish.

SKILL RATING: ●

YARN AND MATERIALS

James C Brett Flutterby Chunky (100% polyester) chunky (bulky) weight yarn, approx. 175m (191yd) per 100g (3½oz) ball

    1 ball each of:
    White B1 (A)
    Gold B51 (B)
    Small amount of Oatmeal B28
        for nose

Toy safety eyes

Child-safe toy stuffing (fibrefill)

HOOK AND EQUIPMENT

5.5mm (US size I/9) hook

Stitch marker

Yarn needle

FINISHED MEASUREMENTS

33cm (13in) square

TENSION (GAUGE)

12 sts x 6 rows measure 10cm (4in) working treble, using 5.5mm (US size I/9) hook.

ABBREVIATIONS

See page 126.

Make it yours

Create a different character by working in different colours and changing the features – why not try a cuddly cat or sweet puppy?

TIPS Be sure that the tension for the character's head is firm, so that the stuffing will not escape through the stitches.

The Fox has safety eyes – these are secured with locking backs affixed to the inside of the head. You may wish to swap the plastic eyes for stitched features to reduce any hazard for really young children, and take the time to ensure that all elements are sewn or fastened securely.

Mini comfort blanket

Using A, make a magic ring.
Round 1: Ch4 (counts as 1dtr throughout), 3tr into ring, [1dtr into ring, 3tr into ring] 3 times, join with a sl st in top of 4-ch. *(16 sts)*
Round 2: Ch4, 2tr in same st, *1dc in each tr to corner dtr, (2tr, 1dtr, 2tr) in corner dtr; rep from * twice more, 1dc in each tr to end, 2tr in base of 4-ch to finish first corner, join with a sl st in top of 4-ch. *(32 sts – 4 corner dtr + 7 tr per side)*
Round 3: Rep patt set in Round 2. *(48 sts)*
Rounds 4–9: Change to B, cont in patt as set. *(144 sts)*

BORDER

Change to A, ch2 (does not count as a st), *1htr in each st to corner, (1tr, 5dtr, 1tr) in corner; rep from * around, join with a sl st in first st.
Fasten off.

Ears

(make 2)
Using A, make a magic ring.
Round 1: 6dc into ring. *(6 sts)*
Work in a continuous spiral, placing marker for start of round.
Round 2: *dc in next st, 2dc in next st; rep from * to end. *(9 sts)*
Round 3: *1dc in next 2 sts, 2dc in next st; rep from * to end. *(12 sts)*
Round 4: Change to B, *1dc in next 3 sts, 2dc in next st; rep from * to end. *(15 sts)*
Round 5: *1dc in next 4 sts, 2dc in next st; rep from * to end. *(18 sts)*
Round 6: 1dc in each st to end.
Fasten off, leaving a long yarn tail for sewing to head.

Head

Using B, make a magic ring.
Round 1: 6dc in ring. *(6 sts)*
Work in a continuous spiral, placing marker for start of round.
Round 2: 2dc in each st to end. *(12 sts)*
Round 3: *2dc in next st, 1dc in next st; rep from * to end. *(18 sts)*
Round 4: *2dc in next st, 1dc in next 2 sts; rep from * to end. *(24 sts)*
Round 5: *2dc in next st, 1dc in next 3 sts; rep from * to end. *(30 sts)*
Round 6: *2dc in next st, 1dc in next 4 sts; rep from * to end. *(36 sts)*
Round 7: *2dc in next st, 1dc in next 5 sts; rep from * to end. *(42 sts)*
Rounds 8–11: Change to A, 1dc in each st to end.
Rounds 12 and 13: 1dc in each st to end.
Round 14: *Dc2tog, 1dc in next 5 sts; rep from * to end. *(36 sts)*
Round 15: *Dc2tog, 1dc in next 4 sts; rep from * to end. *(30 sts)*
Flatten the ears and sew them into position on side of head.
Round 16: *Dc2tog, 1dc in next 3 sts; rep from * to end. *(24 sts)*
Embroider nose and add safety eyes. Stuff lightly.
Round 17: *Dc2tog, 1dc in next 2 sts; rep from * to end. *(18 sts)*
Round 18: *Dc2tog, 1dc in next st; rep from * to end. *(12 sts)*
Complete stuffing.
Round 19: *Dc2tog; rep from * to end. *(6 sts)*
Fasten off.

Making up and finishing

Sew the head securely to the middle of the blanket. Weave in ends (see page 123), knotting the tail of the chenille yarn to prevent fraying.

Fun Fruit

These amigurumi-style fruits are the perfect addition to a play kitchen or food set. Worked in a bright, colourful yarn, they look good enough to eat!

SKILL RATING: ●●

YARN AND MATERIALS

Sirdar Happy Cotton (100% cotton) DK (light worsted) weight yarn, approx. 43m (47yd) per 20g (¾oz) ball
  1 ball each of:
  Juicy 792 (orange) (A)
  Treetop 780 (green) (B)
  Ketchup 790 (red) (C)
  Biscuit 776 (light brown) (D)

Child-safe toy stuffing (fibrefill)

HOOK AND EQUIPMENT

4mm (US size G/6) hook

Stitch marker

Yarn needle

FINISHED MEASUREMENTS

Satsuma: 4.5cm (1¾in) tall

Apple: 5cm (2in) tall

Pear: 9.5cm (3¾in) tall

TENSION (GAUGE)

Not applicable for this project, crochet to create a firm fabric.

ABBREVIATIONS

See page 126.

Make it yours

These can be easily scaled up by selecting a larger hook and a heavier weight yarn. Be sure that the crochet fabric is dense enough so that the stuffing doesn't leak out.

Satsuma

Using A, make a magic ring.
Round 1: 6dc into ring. *(6 sts)*
Work in a continuous spiral, placing marker for start of round.
Round 2: 2dc in each st to end. *(12 sts)*
Round 3: [2dc in next st, 1dc in next st] 6 times. *(18 sts)*
Round 4: [2dc in next st, 1dc in next 2 sts] 6 times. *(24 sts)*
Weave in yarn end from magic ring.
Round 5: [2dc in next st, 1dc in next 3 sts] 6 times. *(30 sts)*
Round 6: [2dc in next st, 1dc in next 4 sts] 6 times. *(36 sts)*
Rounds 7–11: 1dc in each st to end.
Begin stuffing the fruit.
Round 12: [Dc2tog, 1dc in next 4 sts] 6 times. *(30 sts)*
Round 13: [Dc2tog, 1dc in next 3 sts] 6 times. *(24 sts)*
Round 14: [Dc2tog, 1dc in next 2 sts] 6 times. *(18 sts)*
Round 15: [Dc2tog, 1dc in next st] 6 times. *(12 sts)*
Finish stuffing fruit firmly.
Round 16: [Dc2tog] 6 times. *(6 sts)*
Round 17: [Dc2tog] 3 times. *(3 sts)*
Cut the yarn and weave through the stitches, draw up to close the hole and fasten off.

Making up and finishing

With a yarn needle and B, make a cross stitch (see page 125) and knot over the base of the fruit, working over the centre point of the magic ring. Bring the yarn through the middle of the fruit and draw up slightly to create the shaping. Work a cross stitch and knot over the centre top and knot securely, bury the yarn tails and fasten off.

Apple

Using C, make a magic ring.
Round 1: 6dc into ring. *(6 sts)*
Work in a continuous spiral, placing marker for start of round.
Round 2: 2dc in each st to end. *(12 sts)*
Round 3: [2dc in next st, 1dc in next st] 6 times. *(18 sts)*
Round 4: [2dc in next st, 1dc in next 2 sts] 6 times. *(24 sts)*
Round 5: 1dc in each st to end.
Weave in yarn end from magic ring.
Round 6: [2dc in next st, 1dc in next 3 sts] 6 times. *(30 sts)*
Rounds 7 and 8: 1dc in each st to end.
Round 9: [2dc in next st, 1dc in next 4 sts] 6 times. *(36 sts)*
Rounds 10–12: 1dc in each st to end.
Begin stuffing fruit.
Round 13: [Dc2tog, 1dc in next 4 sts] 6 times. *(30 sts)*
Round 14: 1dc in each st to end.
Round 15: [Dc2tog, 1dc in next 3 sts] 6 times. *(24 sts)*
Round 16: [Dc2tog, 1dc in next 2 sts] 6 times. *(18 sts)*
Round 17: [Dc2tog, 1dc in next st] 6 times. *(12 sts)*
Finish stuffing fruit firmly.
Round 18: [Dc2tog] 6 times. *(6 sts)*
Cut the yarn and weave through the stitches, draw up to close the hole and fasten off.

LEAF

Using B, ch5.

Row 1: 1dc in 2nd ch from hook, 1dc in next ch, 1htr in next ch, 5htr in last ch, rotate work and cont along second side of chain, 1htr in next ch, 1dc in next ch, join with a sl st in first st.

Fasten off, leaving a long tail to sew to fruit.

Making up and finishing

Join in D at top of fruit, ch7, sl st in 2nd ch from hook and in each ch to end to create the stalk.

Cut the yarn leaving a long tail, and thread onto a yarn needle. Bring the yarn through the centre of the fruit and draw up slightly to create the shaping. Work a cross stitch (see page 125) and knot over the centre point of the magic ring and knot securely, then bury the yarn tails and fasten off.

Sew the leaf into position on the top of the fruit.

Pear

Using B, make a magic ring.

Round 1: 6dc into ring. *(6 sts)*

Work in a continuous spiral, placing marker for start of round.

Round 2: 2dc in each st to end. *(12 sts)*

Round 3: [2dc in next st, 1dc in next st] 6 times. *(18 sts)*

Round 4: [2dc in next st, 1dc in next 2 sts] 6 times. *(24 sts)*

Round 5: 1dc in each st to end.

Weave in yarn end from magic ring.

Round 6: [2dc in next st, 1dc in next 3 sts] 6 times. *(30 sts)*

Round 7: 1dc in each st to end.

Round 8: [2dc in next st, 1dc in next 4 sts] 6 times. *(36 sts)*

Rounds 9–11: 1dc in each st to end.

Begin stuffing fruit.

Round 12: [Dc2tog, 1dc in next 4 sts] 6 times. *(30 sts)*

Rounds 13 and 14: 1dc in each st to end.

Round 15: [Dc2tog, 1dc in next 3 sts] 6 times. *(24 sts)*

Round 16: [Dc2tog, 1dc in next 2 sts] 6 times. *(18 sts)*

Rounds 17–20: 1dc in each st to end.

Round 21: [Dc2tog, 1dc in next st] 6 times. *(12 sts)*

Rounds 22 and 23: 1dc in each st to end.

Finish stuffing fruit firmly.

Round 24: [Dc2tog] 6 times. *(6 sts)*

Round 25: [Dc2tog] 3 times. *(3 sts)*

Cut the yarn and weave through the stitches, draw up to close the hole and fasten off.

TIPS The fruits are given a plush finish with the use of toy filling – check that the stuffing selected is a child-safe brand. Alternatively, if you have lots and lots of yarn ends they can be great for filling in small areas – but you will need a lot for a firm finish!

These projects are worked in the round, a locking stitch marker – or a safety pin – is a great way to mark the first stitch of the round and will help you to keep track of the decreases and increases.

Making up and finishing

Join in D at top of fruit, ch7, sl st in 2nd ch from hook and in each ch to end to create the stalk.

Cut the yarn leaving a long tail, and thread onto a yarn needle. Bring the yarn through the centre of the fruit and draw up slightly to create the shaping. Work a cross stitch (see page 125) and knot over the centre point of the magic ring and knot securely, then bury the yarn tails and fasten off.

Amigurumi Teddy Bear

A cuddly teddy is a childhood classic; this toy is created in the amigurumi style, working in rounds and stuffed firmly. Create a colourful scarf with leftover yarns in your favourite colour combinations.

SKILL RATING: ●●

YARN AND MATERIALS

Stylecraft Life DK (75% acrylic, 25% wool) DK (light worsted) weight yarn, approx. 298m (326yd) per 100g (3½oz) ball
  1 ball of Silver Nepp 2499 (A)
Stylecraft Special DK (100% acrylic) DK (light worsted) yarn, approx. 295m (323yd) per 100g (3½oz) ball
  Small amount each of:
  Shrimp 1132 (bright pink) (B)
  Citron 1263 (bright yellow) (C)

Toy safety eyes (or use black yarn)

Small amount of black yarn for face detail

Child-safe toy stuffing (fibrefill)

HOOK AND EQUIPMENT

4mm (US size G/6) hook

Stitch marker

Yarn needle

FINISHED MEASUREMENTS

Teddy: 30.5cm (12in) tall

Scarf: 34.5cm (13½in) excluding tassels

TENSION (GAUGE)

22 sts x 24 rows measure 10cm (4in) working double crochet, using 4mm (US size G/6) hook.

ABBREVIATIONS

See page 126.

Head

Using A, make a magic ring.
Round 1: 6dc into ring. *(6 sts)*
Work in a continuous spiral, placing marker for start of round.
Round 2: 2dc in each st to end. *(12 sts)*
Round 3: [2dc in next st, 1dc in next st] 6 times. *(18 sts)*
Round 4: [2dc in next st, 1dc in next 2 sts] 6 times. *(24 sts)*
Round 5: [2dc in next st, 1dc in next 3 sts] 6 times. *(30 sts)*
Round 6: [2dc in next st, 1dc in next 4 sts] 6 times. *(36 sts)*
Round 7: [2dc in next st, 1dc in next 5 sts] 6 times. *(42 sts)*
Round 8: [2dc in next st, 1dc in next 6 sts] 6 times. *(48 sts)*
Round 9: [2dc in next st, 1dc in next 7 sts] 6 times. *(54 sts)*
Round 10: [2dc in next st, 1dc in next 8 sts] 6 times. *(60 sts)*
Round 11: [2dc in next st, 1dc in next 9 sts] 6 times. *(66 sts)*
Rounds 12–21: 1dc in each st.
Round 22: [Dc2tog, 1dc in next 9 sts] 6 times. *(60 sts)*
Round 23: [Dc2tog, 1dc in next 8 sts] 6 times. *(54 sts)*
Round 24: [Dc2tog, 1dc in next 7 sts] 6 times. *(48 sts)*
Round 25: [Dc2tog, 1dc in next 6 sts] 6 times. *(42 sts)*
Round 26: [Dc2tog, 1dc in next 5 sts] 6 times. *(36 sts)*
Round 27: [Dc2tog, 1dc in next 4 sts] 6 times. *(30 sts)*
Round 28: [Dc2tog, 1dc in next 3 sts] 6 times. *(24 sts)*
Fasten off, leaving a long yarn tail for sewing to the body. Secure toy safety eyes (if using them) or embroider eyes onto bear. Embroider facial features (see page 125).

Ears

(make 2)
Using A, make a magic ring.
Round 1: 10dc into ring. *(10 sts)*
Work in a continuous spiral, placing marker for start of round.
Round 2: 2dc in each st to end. *(20 sts)*
Rounds 3–6: 1dc in each st to end.
Fold in half to make half circle shape. Working through matching sts on both front and back half at same time, work 1sl st in each st to join two sides.

Fasten off, leaving a long yarn tail for sewing to the head. Position ears evenly on sides of head and sew in place, knotting yarn securely on inside.
Fill head firmly with toy stuffing.

Legs

(make 2)
Using A, make a magic ring.
Round 1: 6dc into ring. *(6 sts)*
Work in a continuous spiral, placing marker for start of round.
Round 2: 2dc in each st to end. *(12 sts)*
Round 3: [2dc in next st, 1dc in next st] 6 times. *(18 sts)*
Round 4: [2dc in next st, 1dc in next 2 sts] 6 times. *(24 sts)*
Round 5: [2dc in next st, 1dc in next 3 sts] 6 times. *(30 sts)*
Round 6: 1dcBLO in each st to end.
Rounds 7–21: 1dc in each st to end.
Fasten off and weave in ends.
Rep to make second leg, don't cut yarn but cont to work body.

BODY

Cont working in rounds and hold second leg next to first one.
Ch4, join in start of second leg with sl st, 1dc in next 29 sts around leg, 1dc in each st of 4-ch, 1dc in next 29 sts around next leg, 1dc in each st on second side of 4-ch, back to start of round. *(66 sts)*
Place marker for start of round.
Round 1: 1dc in each st to end.
Round 2: [2dc in next st, 1dc in next 10 sts] 6 times. *(72 sts)*
Round 3: [2dc in next st, 1dc in next 11 sts] 6 times. *(78 sts)*
Round 4: [2dc in next st, 1dc in next 12 sts] 6 times. *(84 sts)*
Rounds 5–8: 1dc in each st to end.
Round 9: [Dc2tog, 1dc in next 12 sts] 6 times. *(78 sts)*
Rounds 10 and 11: 1dc in each st to end.
Round 12: [Dc2tog, 1dc in next 11 sts] 6 times. *(72 sts)*
Rounds 13 and 14: 1dc in each st to end.
Round 15: [Dc2tog, 1dc in next 10 sts] 6 times. *(66 sts)*

Round 16: 1dc in each st to end.
Round 17: [Dc2tog, 1dc in next 9 sts] 6 times. *(60 sts)*
Round 18: 1dc in each st to end.
Round 19: [Dc2tog, 1dc in next 8 sts] 6 times. *(54 sts)*
Round 20: 1dc in each st to end.
Round 21: [Dc2tog, 1dc in next 16 sts] 3 times. *(51 sts)*
Round 22: 1dc in each st to end.
Begin stuffing lower portion of bear, ensuring that stuffing is pushed down firmly into legs.
Round 23: [Dc2tog, 1dc in next 15 sts] 3 times. *(48 sts)*
Round 24: 1dc in each st to end.
Round 25: [Dc2tog, 1dc in next 14 sts] 3 times. *(45 sts)*
Round 26: [Dc2tog, 1dc in next 13 sts] 3 times. *(42 sts)*
Round 27: [Dc2tog, 1dc in next 12 sts] 3 times. *(39 sts)*
Round 28: [Dc2tog, 1dc in next 11 sts] 3 times. *(36 sts)*
Round 29: [Dc2tog, 1dc in next 10 sts] 3 times. *(33 sts)*
Round 30: 1dc in each st to end.
Round 31: [Dc2tog, 1dc in next 9 sts] 3 times. *(30 sts)*
Round 32: 1dc in each st to end.
Round 33: [Dc2tog, 1dc in next 8 sts] 3 times. *(27 sts)*
Round 34: [Dc2tog, 1dc in next 7 sts] 3 times. *(24 sts)*
Fasten off. Add toy stuffing to fill out body firmly.

TIPS The stitches for amigurumi need to be fairly tight to create the firm fabric that prevents the stuffing from coming out. Work a swatch before starting the bear and select a smaller or larger hook to get a snug tension.

This bear has safety eyes – these are secured with locking backs affixed to the inside of the head. You may wish to swap the plastic eyes for stitched features to reduce any hazard for really young children.

Arms

(make 2)
Using A, make a magic ring.
Round 1: 6dc into ring. *(6 sts)*
Work in a continuous spiral, placing marker for start
of round.
Round 2: 2dc in each st to end. *(12 sts)*
Round 3: [2dc in next st, 1dc in next st] 6 times. *(18 sts)*
Round 4: 1dcBLO in each st to end.
Rounds 5–16: 1dc in each st to end.
Round 17: Dc2tog, 1dc in each st to end. *(17 sts)*
Round 18: 1dc in each st to end.
Round 19: Dc2tog, 1dc in each st to end. *(16 sts)*
Round 20: 1dc in each st to end.
Round 21: Dc2tog, 1dc in each st to end. *(15 sts)*
Round 22: 1dc in each st to end.
Round 23: Dc2tog, 1dc in each st to end. *(14 sts)*
Round 24: 1dc in each st to end.
Round 25: Dc2tog, 1dc in each st to end. *(13 sts)*
Round 26: Dc2tog, 1dc in each st to end. *(12 sts)*
Stuff arms.
Fasten off, leaving a long yarn tail for sewing to body.

Scarf

Using B, ch6.
Row 1: 1dc in 2nd ch from hook, 1dc in each ch to end.
(5 sts)
Rows 2–5: Ch1 (does not count as a st throughout),
1dc in each st to end, turn.
Rows 6–10: Change to C, ch1, 1dc in each st to end,
turn.
Rows 11–15: Change to B, ch1, 1dc in each st to end,
turn.
Rows 16–20: Change to C, ch1, 1dc in each st to end,
turn.
Rep Rows 11–20 three more times.
Rows 51–55: Change to B, ch1, 1dc in each st, turn.
Fasten off.

Making up and finishing

Position ears evenly on sides of head and sew in place,
knotting yarn securely on inside.
Fill head firmly with toy stuffing.
Place the head onto the opening at the body and
sew securely into place. Add more stuffing at the
neck as needed.
Place the arms under the neck section of bear, ensuring
they are evenly spaced, and sew securely into place,
flattening the top of the arms.
Cut eighteen 10cm (4in) lengths of C. Fold three strands
double, thread the loop through the first stitch on the
end of the scarf and then pull the ends through the loop
to make a lark's head knot (see page 126). Rep to add
three tassels to each end of the scarf. Trim to neaten.
Wrap scarf around bear's neck.
Weave in all ends neatly (see page 123).

Make it yours

This bear is worked in a single colour of yarn, but you
can adapt the look by changing colours, or by making
the flat circles at the base of the arms and legs in
a contrast shade.

Sleepy Swaddle Baby

This pocket-sized doll is ideal for little hands. The simple shape and sleepy face will make this a bedtime favourite.

SKILL RATING: ●

YARN AND MATERIALS

Rico Creative Cotton Aran (100% cotton) aran (worsted) weight yarn, approx. 85m (93yd) per 50g (1¾oz) ball
    1 ball each of:
    Smokey Berry 12 (dusky pink) (A)
    Smokey Pink 06 (pale pink) (B)

Small amount of black yarn for eye detail

Child-safe toy stuffing (fibrefill)

HOOK AND EQUIPMENT

4mm (US size G/6) hook

Stitch marker

Yarn needle

FINISHED MEASUREMENTS

19cm (7½in) tall

TENSION (GAUGE)

Not applicable for this project, crochet to create a firm fabric.

ABBREVIATIONS

See page 126.

Body

Using A, make a magic ring.
Round 1: 6dc into ring. *(6 sts)*
Work in a continuous spiral, placing marker for start of round.
Round 2: 2dc in each st to end. *(12 sts)*
Round 3: [2dc in next st, 1dc in next st] 6 times. *(18 sts)*
Round 4: [2dc in next st, 1dc in next 2 sts] 6 times. *(24 sts)*
Round 5: [2dc in next st, 1dc in next 3 sts] 6 times. *(30 sts)*
Round 6: [2dc in next st, 1dc in next 4 sts] 6 times. *(36 sts)*
Rounds 7–10: 1dc in each st to end.
Round 11: [Dc2tog, 1dc in next 4 sts] 6 times. *(30 sts)*
Rounds 12–15: 1dc in each st to end.
Round 16: [Dc2tog, 1dc in next 3 sts] 6 times. *(24 sts)*
Rounds 17–20: 1dc in each st to end.
Round 21: [Dc2tog, 1dc in next 2 sts] 6 times. *(18 sts)*
Round 22: 1dc in each st to end.
Round 23: [Dc2tog, 1dc in next st] 6 times. *(12 sts)*
Fasten off, leaving a long yarn tail. Stuff firmly.

Head

Using B, make a magic ring.
Round 1: 6dc into ring. *(6 sts)*
Work in a continuous spiral, placing marker for start of round.
Round 2: 2dc in each st to end. *(12 sts)*
Round 3: [2dc in next st, 1dc in next st] 6 times. *(18 sts)*
Round 4: [2dc in next st, 1dc in next 2 sts] 6 times. *(24 sts)*
Round 5: [2dc in next st, 1dc in next 3 sts] 6 times. *(30 sts)*
Round 6: [2dc in next st, 1dc in next 4 sts] 6 times. *(36 sts)*
Rounds 7–10: 1dc in each st to end.
Round 11: [Dc2tog, 1dc in next 4 sts] 6 times. *(30 sts)*
With black yarn and yarn needle, embroider eye details to face.
Round 12: [Dc2tog, 1dc in next 3 sts] 6 times. *(24 sts)*
Round 13: [Dc2tog, 1dc in next 2 sts] 6 times. *(18 sts)*
Round 14: [Dc2tog, 1dc in next st] 6 times. *(12 sts)*
Fasten off, leaving a long yarn tail. Stuff firmly.

Make it yours

These dolls can be worked in any colour or selection of colours you choose. The simple shaping of the body of the doll makes it a great blank canvas for variegated or self-striping yarns.

TIPS This project is worked in the round, a locking stitch marker – or a safety pin – is a great way to mark the first stitch of the round and will help you to keep track of the decreases and increases.

The eyes are stitched onto the surface of the doll's head. Use the stitches as a guide for placement to get even details.

Arms

(make 2)

Using B, make a magic ring.

Round 1: 6dc into ring. *(6 sts)*

Work in a continuous spiral, placing marker for start of round.

Round 2: 2dc in each st to end. *(12 sts)*

Round 3: 1dc in each st to end.

Round 4: Change to A, 1dcBLO in each st to end.

Round 5: Dc2tog, 1dc in each st to end. *(11 sts)*

Round 6: Dc2tog, 1dc in each st to end. *(10 sts)*

Rounds 7–12: 1dc in each st to end.

Fasten off, leaving a long yarn tail. Lightly stuff.

Bonnet

Using B, ch31.

Row 1: 1dc in 2nd ch from hook and each ch to end, turn. *(30 sts)*

Rows 2–7: Ch2 (does not count as a st), 1htr in each st to end, turn.

Fasten off, leaving a long yarn tail. Thread tail onto a yarn needle, fold long edge in half and seam to make back of bonnet.

Making up and finishing

Place the head onto the opening at the body and sew securely into place using the yarn tails. Add more stuffing at the neck as needed. Place the arms at the top of the body, ensuring they are evenly spaced, and sew securely into place, flattening the top of the arms. Place the bonnet over the head and sew around the neck to secure.

Dotty Cubes

Stacking cubes not only look wonderful as a design accent to a baby's nursery, they are fun first toys for little ones too. These cubes feature a dot motif granny square to create a bold focal point to each side.

SKILL RATING: ● ●

YARN AND MATERIALS

Stylecraft Special DK (100% acrylic) DK (light worsted) weight yarn, approx. 295m (323yd) per 100g (3½oz) ball
1 ball each of:
Lincoln 1834 (pale green) (A)
Citron 1263 (yellow) (B)
Lavender 1188 (lavender blue) (C)
Powder Pink 1843 (pale pink) (D)
Shrimp 1132 (bright pink) (E)
Cloud Blue 1019 (pale blue) (F)
A Hint of Silver 1807 (grey-white) (G)

Child-safe toy stuffing (fibrefill)

HOOK AND EQUIPMENT

4mm (US size G/6) hook

Plastic canvas sheets (as used in needlecraft)

Yarn needle

FINISHED MEASUREMENTS

12cm (4¾in) cube

TENSION (GAUGE)

Each dot motif granny square measures 10cm (4in) using 4mm (US size G/6) hook.

ABBREVIATIONS

See page 126.

TIPS Plastic canvas sheets – commonly found in the needlecraft section of the craft store – are handy for adding more solid structure to projects. They can be trimmed to size and help items, like these cubes, hold their shape. Once trimmed to size, be sure to round off any sharp points on the corners.

Blocking the square helps to give each piece a neat straight edge and ensures they are all the same size. This will make the construction of the cubes easier; the addition of the plastic canvas will also help to hold the pieces in shape.

Squares

(make 1 with dot in each of A, B, C, D, E and F per cube)
Using first colour, make a magic ring.
Round 1: Ch3 into ring (counts as 1tr throughout), 11tr into ring, join with a sl st in top of 3-ch. *(12 sts)*
Round 2: Ch3, 1tr in same st, 2tr in next 11 sts, join with a sl st in top of 3-ch. *(24 sts)*
Round 3: Ch3, 1tr in same st, [1tr in next st, 2tr in next st] 11 times, 1tr in next st, join with a sl st in top of 3-ch. *(36 sts)*
Fasten off.
Round 4: Join G to any st, ch3, 1tr in same st, *1tr in next st, 1htr in next 2 sts, 1dc in next 2 sts, 1htr in next 2 sts, 1tr in next st, (2tr, ch2, 2tr) in next st (corner); rep from * twice more, 1tr in next st, 1htr in next 2 sts, 1dc in next 2 sts, 1htr in next 2 sts, 1tr in next st, 2tr in same sp as first sts, ch2, join with a sl st in top of 3-ch. *(48 sts)*
Round 5: Ch3, 1tr in next 11 sts, (1tr, ch2, 1tr) in corner ch sp, *1tr in next 12 sts, (1tr, ch2, tr) in corner ch sp; rep from * twice more, join with a sl st in top of 3-ch. *(56 sts)*
Fasten off.

Making up and finishing

Block squares to size and weave in all ends (see page 123). Place one square in the centre and one at each side, then place the last square to align with the top of one square around the centre. Working with the centre square and one side square in turn, align the sides with WS together. Using G, seam the pieces together with slip stitch to make cube shape. Before working the final seam, trim the plastic canvas into six 10cm (4in) squares and slide inside the shape on the inside of each square. Before adding the final piece of plastic canvas, stuff lightly. Position the last piece of plastic canvas and seam the final edge closed.
Weave in all ends.

Make it yours

This project can be made larger simply by working in a chunkier yarn and using a larger hook. Remember to increase the amount of plastic canvas and stuffing to suit.

Cuddly Lion

Jungle animals are a really popular theme for a nursery; this cuddly lion will look just the part in baby's room.

SKILL RATING: ● ●

YARN AND MATERIALS

Rico Creative Cotton Aran (100% cotton) aran (worsted) weight yarn, approx. 85m (93yd) per 50g (1¾oz) ball
   2 balls of Corn 25 (gold) (A)
   1 ball each of:
   Buttercream 24 (pale gold) (B)
   Mustard 70 (C)
   Emerald 69 (D)

Small amount of brown yarn for face detail

Child-safe toy stuffing (fibrefill)

Toy safety eyes (optional)

HOOK AND EQUIPMENT

4mm (US size G/6) hook

Stitch marker

Yarn needle

FINISHED MEASUREMENTS

25.5cm (10in) tall

TENSION (GAUGE)

Not applicable for this project, crochet to create a firm fabric.

ABBREVIATIONS

See page 126.

SPECIAL ABBREVIATION

BS (bobble stitch): *yarn round hook, insert hook in stitch, yarn round hook and pull through a loop (3 loops on hook), yarn round hook and pull through 2 loops (2 loops on hook); rep from * 4 more times in same stitch (6 loops on hook), yarn round hook, pull through all loops, ch1 to secure bobble.

Mane

Using C, ch8.
Row 1: 1dc in 2nd ch from hook and each st to end, turn. *(7 sts)*
Row 2: Ch1 (does not count as a st throughout), 1dc in first st, BS, 1dc in next st, BS, 1dc in next st, BS, 1dc in next st, turn.
Row 3: Ch1, 1dc in next 2 sts, BS, 1dc in next st, BS, 1dc in next 2 sts, turn.
Rep Rows 2 and 3 a further 12 times, then rep Row 2 only once more.
Next row: Ch1, 1dc in each st to end.
Fasten off and set aside.

Ears

(make 2)
Using A, make a magic ring.
Round 1: 6dc into ring. *(6 sts)*
Row 1: Ch2 (counts as 1htr), 1htr in same st, 2htr in each st to end, turn. *(12 sts)*
Row 2: Change to B, 1dc in each st to end.
Fasten off and set aside.

Head

Using B, make a magic ring.
Round 1: 6dc into ring. *(6 sts)*
Work in a continuous spiral, placing marker for start of round.
Round 2: 2dc in each st to end. *(12 sts)*
Round 3: *1dc in next st, 2dc in next st; rep from * to end. *(18 sts)*
Round 4: *1dc in next 2 sts, 2dc in next st; rep from * to end. *(24 sts)*
Weave in yarn end from magic ring.
Round 5: *1dc in next 3 sts, 2dc in next st; rep from * to end. *(30 sts)*
Round 6: *1dc in next 4 sts, 2dc in next st; rep from * to end. *(36 sts)*
Round 7: *1dc in next 5 sts, 2dc in next st; rep from * to end. *(42 sts)*
Round 8: *1dc in next 6 sts, 2dc in next st; rep from * to end. *(48 sts)*
Round 9: *1dc in next 7 sts, 2dc in next st; rep from * to end. *(54 sts)*

TIPS When filling smaller areas like the arms and legs, a pair of hemostat forceps are useful to get the stuffing into the smaller spaces. Alternatively, use a chopstick or the wrong end of a pencil to push small pieces in at a time.

The lion has safety eyes – these are secured with locking backs affixed to the inside of the head. You may wish to swap the plastic eyes for stitched features to reduce any hazard for really young children.

Round 10: *1dc in next 8 sts, 2dc in next st; rep from * to end. *(60 sts)*
Rounds 11–18: Change to A, 1dc in each st to end.
Round 19: Change to C, *1dc in next 8 sts, dc2tog; rep from * to end. *(54 sts)*
Round 20: *1dc in next 7 sts, dc2tog; rep from * to end. *(48 sts)*
Round 21: *1dc in next 6 sts, dc2tog; rep from * to end. *(42 sts)*
With magic ring in middle, begin sewing on features. Apply safety eyes, or sew eyes in position. Embroider nose and mouth. Place ears at colour change and sew in place. Weave in all ends.
Begin stuffing head.
Round 22: *1dc in next 4 sts, dc2tog; rep from * to end. *(35 sts)*
Cont stuffing while working rounds.
Round 23: *1dc in next 3 sts, dc2tog; rep from * to end. *(28 sts)*
Round 24: *1dc in next 2 sts, dc2tog; rep from * to end. *(21 sts)*
Finish stuffing head.
Round 25: *1dc in next st, dc2tog; rep from * to end. *(14 sts)*
Round 27: [Dc2tog] to end. *(7 sts)*
Round 28: 1dc in first st, [dc2tog] to end. *(4 sts)*
Cut the yarn and weave through the stitches, draw up to close the hole and fasten off.

Body

Using A, make a magic ring.
Round 1: 6dc into ring. *(6 sts)*
Work in a continuous spiral, placing marker for start of round.
Round 2: 2dc in each st to end. *(12 sts)*
Round 3: *1dc in next st, 2dc in next st; rep from * to end. *(18 sts)*
Round 4: *1dc in next 2 sts, 2dc in next st; rep from * to end. *(24 sts)*
Round 5: *1dc in next 3 sts, 2dc in next st; rep from * to end. *(30 sts)*
Round 6: *1dc in next 4 sts, 2dc in next st; rep from * to end. *(36 sts)*
Round 7: *1dc in next 5 sts, 2dc in next st; rep from * to end. *(42 sts)*
Round 8: *1dc in next 6 sts, 2dc in next st; rep from * to end. *(48 sts)*
Round 9: *1dc in next 7 sts, 2dc in next st; rep from * to end. *(54 sts)*
Round 10: *1dc in next 8 sts, 2dc in next st; rep from * to end. *(60 sts)*
Round 11: *1dc in next 9 sts, 2dc in next st; rep from * to end. *(66 sts)*
Round 12: 1dcBLO in each st to end.
Round 13: *1dc in next 10 sts, 2dc in next st; rep from * to end. *(72 sts)*
Rounds 14–16: 1dc in each st to end.
Round 17: *1dc in next 10 sts, dc2tog; rep from * to end. *(66 sts)*
Round 18: 1dc in each st to end.
Round 19: *1dc in next 9 sts, dc2tog; rep from * to end. *(60 sts)*
Rounds 20 and 21: 1dc in each st to end.
Round 22: *1dc in next 8 sts, dc2tog; rep from * to end. *(54 sts)*
Rounds 23–25: 1dc in each st to end.
Round 26: *1dc in next 7 sts, dc2tog; rep from * to end. *(48 sts)*
Rounds 27 and 28: 1dc in each st to end.
Round 29: *1dc in next 6 sts, dc2tog; rep from * to end. *(42 sts)*
Round 30: 1dc in each st to end.
Round 31: *1dc in next 5 sts, dc2tog; rep from * to end. *(36 sts)*
Round 32: 1dc in each st to end.
Round 33: *1dc in next 4 sts, dc2tog; rep from * to end. *(30 sts)*
Round 34: *1dc in next 3 sts, dc2tog; rep from * to end. *(24 sts)*
Fasten off, leaving a long yarn tail to sew to head.
Stuff firmly.

Arms

(make 2)

Using A, make a magic ring.

Round 1: 6dc into ring. *(6 sts)*

Work in a continuous spiral, placing marker for start of round.

Round 2: 2dc in each st to end. *(12 sts)*

Rounds 3–15: 1dc in each st to end.

Fasten off, leaving a long tail for sewing onto body. Lightly stuff.

Legs

(make 2)

Using B, ch5.

Round 1: 1dc in 2nd ch from hook, 1dc in next 2 ch, 3dc in last ch, rotate work and cont along second side of chain, 1dc in next 3 ch, 3dc in last ch. *(12 sts)*

Work in a continuous spiral, placing marker for start of round.

Round 2: 1dc in next 3 sts, 2dc in next 3 sts, 1dc in next 3 sts, 2dc in next 3 sts. *(18 sts)*

Round 3: 1dc in each st to end.

Round 4: Change to A, 1dcBLO in each st to end.

Round 5: [1dc in next 3 sts, dc2tog] 3 times, 1dc in next 3 sts. *(15 sts)*

Round 6: *1dc in next 3 sts, dc2tog; rep from * to end. *(12 sts)*

Round 7: 1dc in next 4 sts, [dc2tog] twice, 1dc in next 4 sts. *(10 sts)*

Rounds 8–15: 1dc in each st to end. *(10 sts)*

Fasten off, leaving a long yarn tail to sew to body. Lightly stuff.

Bandana

Using D, ch3.

Row 1: 1dc in 2nd ch from hook, 1dc in next ch, turn. *(2 sts)*

Row 2: Ch1 (does not count as a st throughout), 2dc in each st to end, turn. *(4 sts)*

Row 3: Ch1, 2dc in first st, 1dc in next 2 sts, 2dc in last st, turn. *(6 sts)*

Row 4: Ch1, 2dc in first st, 1dc in next 4 sts, 2dc in last st, turn. *(8 sts)*

Row 5: Ch1, 2dc in first st, 1dc in next 6 sts, 2dc in last st, turn. *(10 sts)*

Row 6: Ch1, 2dc in first st, 1dc in next 8 sts, 2dc in last st, turn. *(12 sts)*

- -

Make it yours

Create the bandana in any colour you like to give the lion a custom finish.

- -

Row 7: Ch1, 2dc in first st, 1dc in next 10 sts, 2dc in last st, turn. *(14 sts)*

Row 8: Ch1, 2dc in first st, 1dc in next 12 sts, 2dc in last st, turn. *(16 sts)*

Row 9: Ch1, 2dc in first st, 1dc in next 14 sts, 2dc in last st, turn. *(18 sts)*

Row 10: Do not cut yarn, ch11, 1dc in 2nd ch from hook, 1dc in next 9 ch, sl st in next 18 sts across bandana.

Fasten off, leaving a long yarn tail to sew on.

Making up and finishing

Place the mane onto the top of the head, aligning with the colour change, and sew securely into place, adding stuffing as you go.

Position the head onto the opening at the body and sew in place, adding more stuffing into the neck space as needed.

Place the arms at the side of the upper body, ensuring they are level, and sew into position, flattening the top of the arms.

Place the legs onto the base of the body, spacing them evenly, and sew into position, flattening the top of the legs.

Place the bandana around the lion's neck and use the yarn end to secure into place at the back.

Weave in all ends (see page 123).

Techniques

In this section, you'll find all the simple crochet and finishing techniques that you'll need to make the projects in this book.

Holding the hook

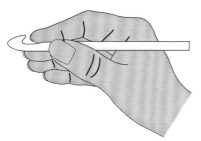

Pick up your hook as though you are picking up a pen or pencil. Keeping the hook held loosely between your fingers and thumb, turn your hand so that the palm is facing up and the hook is balanced in your hand and resting in the space between your index finger and your thumb.

You can also hold the hook like a knife – this may be easier if you are working with a large hook or with chunky yarn. Choose the method that you find most comfortable.

Holding the yarn

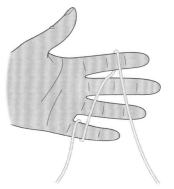

1 Pick up the yarn with your little finger in the opposite hand to your hook, with your palm facing upward and with the short end in front. Turn your hand to face downward, with the yarn on top of your index finger and under the other two fingers and wrapped right around the little finger, as shown above.

2 Turn your hand to face you, ready to hold the work in your middle finger and thumb. Keeping your index finger only at a slight curve, hold the work or the slip knot using the same hand, between your middle finger and your thumb and just below the crochet hook and loop/s on the hook.

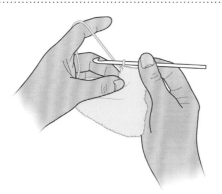

Holding the hook and yarn while crocheting

Keep your index finger, with the yarn draped over it, at a slight curve, and hold your work (or the slip knot) using the same hand, between your middle finger and your thumb and just below the crochet hook and loop/s on the hook.

As you draw the loop through the hook release the yarn on the index finger to allow the loop to stay loose on the hook. If you tense your index finger, the yarn will become too tight and pull the loop on the hook too tight for you to draw the yarn through.

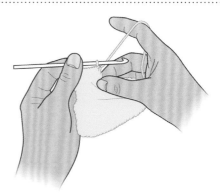

Holding the hook and yarn for left-handers

Some left-handers learn to crochet like right-handers, but others learn with everything reversed – with the hook in the left hand and the yarn in the right.

Making a slip knot

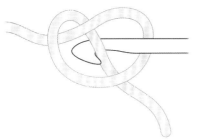

1 In one hand hold the circle at the top where the yarn crosses, and let the tail drop down at the back so that it falls across the centre of the loop. With your free hand or the tip of a crochet hook, pull a loop through the circle.

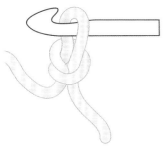

2 Put the hook into the loop and pull gently so that it forms a loose loop on the hook.

Yarn round hook

To create a stitch, catch the yarn from behind with the hook pointing upward. As you gently pull the yarn through the loop on the hook, turn the hook so it faces downward and slide the yarn through the loop. The loop on the hook should be kept loose enough for the hook to slide through easily.

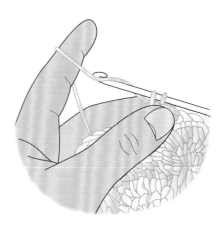

Magic ring

This is a useful starting technique if you do not want a visible hole in the centre of your round. Loop the yarn around your finger, insert the hook through the ring, yarn round hook, pull through the ring to make the first chain. Work the number of stitches required into the ring and then pull the end to tighten the centre ring and close the hole.

Chain

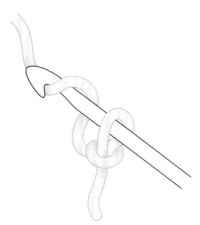

1 Using the hook, wrap the yarn round the hook ready to pull it through the loop on the hook.

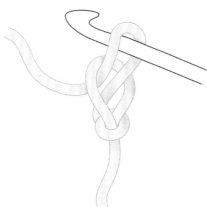

2 Pull through, creating a new loop on the hook. Continue in this way to create a chain of the required length.

Joining a foundation chain to make a ring

If you are crocheting a round shape, one way of starting off is by crocheting a number of chains following the instructions in your pattern, and then joining them into a circle.

 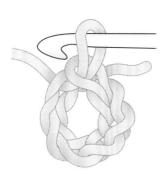

1 To join the chain into a circle, insert the crochet hook into the first chain that you made (not into the slip knot), yarn round hook.

2 Pull the yarn through the chain and through the loop on your hook at the same time, thereby creating a slip stitch and forming a circle. You now have a chain ring ready to work stitches into as instructed in the pattern.

Slip stitch (sl st)

A slip stitch doesn't create any height and is often used as the last stitch to create a smooth and even round or row.

1 To make a slip stitch: first put the hook through the work, yarn round hook.

2 Pull the yarn through both the work and through the loop on the hook at the same time, so you will have 1 loop on the hook.

Making rounds

When working in rounds the work is not turned, so you are always working from one side. Depending on the pattern you are working, a 'round' can be square. Start each round by making one or more chains to create the height you need for the stitch you are working:

Double crochet = 1 chain
Half treble crochet = 2 chains
Treble crochet = 3 chains
Double treble = 4 chains

Work the required stitches to complete the round. At the end of the round, slip stitch into the top of the chain to close the round.

Making rows

When making straight rows you turn the work at the end of each row and make a turning chain to create the height you need for the stitch you are working with, as for making rounds.

Double crochet = 1 chain
Half treble crochet = 2 chains
Treble crochet = 3 chains
Double treble = 4 chains

Continuous spiral

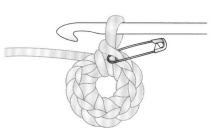

If you work in a spiral you do not need a turning chain. After completing the base ring, place a stitch marker in the first stitch and then continue to crochet around. When you have made a round and reached the point where the stitch marker is, work this stitch, take out the stitch marker from the previous round and put it back into the first stitch of the new round. A safety pin or piece of yarn in a contrasting colour makes a good stitch marker.

Working into top of stitch

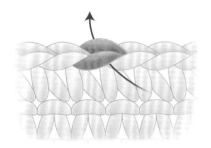

Unless otherwise directed, always insert the hook under both of the two loops on top of the stitch – this is the standard technique.

Working into front loop of stitch (FLO)

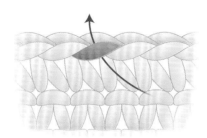

To work into the front loop of a stitch, pick up the front loop from underneath at the front of the work.

Working into back loop of stitch (BLO)

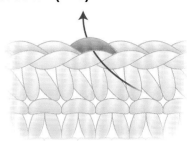

To work into the back loop of the stitch, insert the hook between the front and the back loop, picking up the back loop from the front of the work.

How to measure a tension (gauge) square

Using the hook and the yarn recommended in the pattern, make a number of chains to measure approximately 15cm (6in). Working in the stitch pattern given for the tension measurements, work enough rows to form a square. Fasten off.

Take a ruler, place it horizontally across the square and, using pins, mark a 10cm (4in) area. Repeat vertically to form a 10cm (4in) square on the fabric. Count the number of stitches across, and the number of rows within the square, and compare against the tension given in the pattern.

If your numbers match the pattern then use this size hook and yarn for your project. If you have more stitches, then your tension is tighter than recommended and you need to use a larger hook. If you have fewer stitches, then your tension is looser and you will need a smaller hook.

Make tension squares using different size hooks until you have matched the tension in the pattern, and use this hook to make the project.

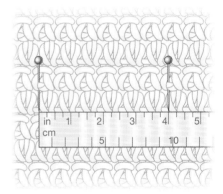

Double crochet (dc)

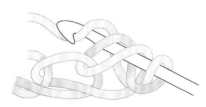

1 Insert the hook into your work, yarn round hook and pull the yarn through the work only. You will then have 2 loops on the hook.

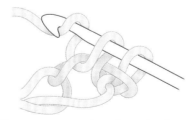

2 Yarn round hook again and pull through the two loops on the hook. You will then have 1 loop on the hook.

Half treble crochet (htr)

1 Before inserting the hook into the work, wrap the yarn round the hook and put the hook through the work with the yarn wrapped around.

2 Yarn round hook again and pull through the first loop on the hook. You now have 3 loops on the hook.

3 Yarn round hook and pull the yarn through all 3 loops. You will be left with 1 loop on the hook.

Treble crochet (tr)

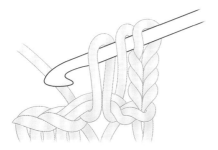  

1 Before inserting the hook into the work, wrap the yarn round the hook. Put the hook through the work with the yarn wrapped around, yarn round hook again and pull through the first loop on the hook. You now have 3 loops on the hook.

2 Yarn round hook again, pull the yarn through the first 2 loops on the hook. You now have 2 loops on the hook.

3 Pull the yarn through 2 loops again. You will be left with 1 loop on the hook.

Double treble crochet (dtr)

Yarn round hook twice, insert the hook into the stitch, yarn round hook, pull a loop through (4 loops on hook), yarn round hook, pull the yarn through 2 stitches (3 loops on hook), yarn round hook, pull a loop through the next 2 stitches (2 loops on hook), yarn round hook, pull a loop through the last 2 stitches. You will be left with 1 loop on the hook.

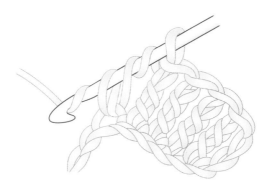

Increasing

Make two or three stitches into one stitch or space from the previous row. The illustration shows a treble crochet increase being made.

Decreasing

You can decrease by either missing the next stitch and continuing to crochet, or by crocheting two or more stitches together. The basic technique for crocheting stitches together is the same, no matter which stitch you are using.

Double crochet two stitches together (dc2tog)

1 Insert the hook into your work, yarn round hook and pull the yarn through the work (2 loops on hook). Insert the hook in next stitch, yarn round hook and pull the yarn through.

2 Yarn round hook again and pull through all 3 loops on the hook. You will then have 1 loop on the hook.

Clusters (CL)

Clusters are groups of stitches, with each stitch only partly worked and then all joined at the end to form one stitch that creates a particular pattern and shape. Shown here is a three-treble cluster, but for four- or five-treble clusters, simply repeat steps 1 and 2 more times.

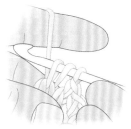

1 Yarn round hook, insert the hook in the stitch (or space). Yarn round hook, pull the yarn through the work (3 loops on hook).

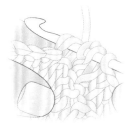

2 Yarn round hook, pull the yarn through 2 of the loops on the hook. Yarn round hook, insert the hook in the same stitch (or space).

3 Yarn round hook, pull the yarn through the work (4 loops on hook). Yarn round hook, pull the yarn through 2 of the loops on the hook (3 loops on hook).

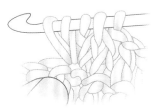

4 Yarn round hook, insert the hook in the same stitch (or space), yarn round hook, pull the yarn through the work (5 loops on hook).

5 Yarn round hook, pull the yarn through 2 of the loops on the hook (4 loops on hook).

6 Yarn round hook, pull the yarn through all 4 loops on the hook (1 loop left on hook). One three-treble cluster made.

Spike stitch

For these stitches you work a normal crochet stitch but into a stitch that is one, two or more rows below, which creates a V of yarn on the surface. They are sometimes called long stitches or extended stitches. These instructions are for an extended double crochet stitch (edc) but the same technique is used for other stitches such as extended treble or extended double treble.

1 Using a contrast yarn, insert your hook into the space one row below the next stitch – this is the top of the stitch one row below, so the same place that the stitch in the previous row is worked.

2 Yarn round hook and draw a loop up so it's level with the original loop on your hook.

3 Yarn round hook and pull through both loops to complete the extended double crochet.

Joining yarn at the end of a row or round

You can use this technique when changing colour, or when joining in a new ball of yarn as one runs out.

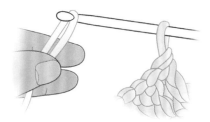

1 Before inserting the hook into the work, wrap the yarn round the hook. Put the hook through the work with the yarn wrapped around, yarn round hook again and pull through the first loop on the hook. You now have 3 loops on the hook.

2 Yarn round hook again, pull the yarn through the first 2 loops on the hook. You now have 2 loops on the hook.

Enclosing a yarn tail

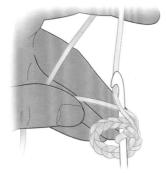

You may find that the yarn tail gets in the way as you work; you can enclose this into the stitches as you go by placing the tail at the back as you wrap the yarn. This also saves having to sew this tail end in later.

Fastening off

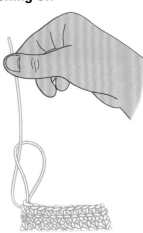

When you have finished crocheting, you need to fasten off the stitches to stop all your work unravelling.
Draw up the final loop of the last stitch to make it bigger. Cut the yarn, leaving a tail of approximately 10cm (4in) – unless a longer end is needed for sewing up. Pull the tail all the way through the loop and pull the loop up tightly.

Joining in new yarn after fastening off

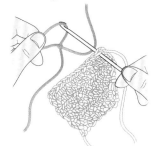

1 Fasten off the old colour (see opposite). Make a slip knot with the new colour (see page 117). Insert the hook into the stitch at the beginning of the next row, then through the slip knot.

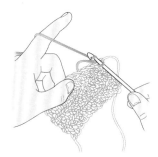

2 Draw the loop of the slip knot through to the front of the work. Carry on working using the new colour, following the instructions in the pattern.

Blocking

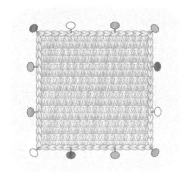

When making garments and toys you will find that taking the time to block and stiffen each crochet element will make a huge difference to the finished effect of your work. Without either of these processes you will find that the crochet will curl out of shape and lose its definition.

For a quick and easy way to block your crochet you'll need blocking pins, some soft foam mats (such as the ones sold as children's play mats) and some ironing spray starch. Pin each item out to shape and size on to the mats and then spray with the starch. Allow to dry for a day before completing your garment or toy.

Weaving in yarn ends

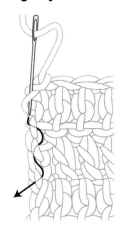

It is important to weave in the tail ends of the yarn so that they are secure and your crochet won't unravel. Thread a yarn needle with the tail end of yarn. On the wrong side, take the needle through the crochet one stitch down on the edge, then take it through the stitches, working in a gentle zigzag. Work through four or five stitches then return in the opposite direction. Remove the needle, pull the crochet gently to stretch it and trim the end.

Double crochet/slip stitch seam

With a double crochet seam you join two pieces together using a crochet hook and working a double crochet stitch through both pieces, instead of sewing them together with a tail of yarn and a yarn sewing needle. This makes a quick and strong seam and gives a slightly raised finish to the edging. For a less raised seam, follow the same basic technique, but work each stitch in slip stitch rather than double crochet.

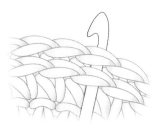

1 Start by lining up the two pieces with wrong sides together. Insert the hook in the top 2 loops of the stitch of the first piece, then into the corresponding stitch on the second piece.

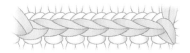

2 Complete the double crochet stitch as normal and continue on the next stitches as directed in the pattern. This gives a raised effect if the double crochet stitches are made on the right side of the work.

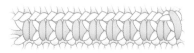

3 You can work with the wrong side of the work facing (with the pieces right side facing) if you don't want this effect and it still creates a good strong join.

Making an oversewn seam

An oversewn join gives a nice flat seam and is the simplest and most common joining technique.

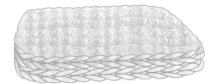

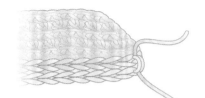

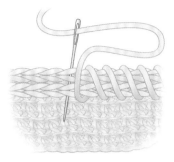

1 Thread a yarn sewing needle with the yarn you're using in the project. Place the pieces to be joined with right sides together.

2 Insert the needle in one corner in the top loops of the stitches of both pieces and pull up the yarn, leaving a tail of about 5cm (2in). Go into the same place with the needle and pull up the yarn again; repeat two or three times to secure the yarn at the start of the seam.

3 Join the pieces together by taking the needle through the loops at the top of corresponding stitches on each piece to the end. Fasten off the yarn at the end, as in step 2.

Join-as-you-go method for granny squares

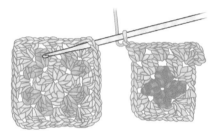

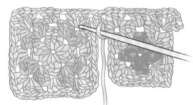

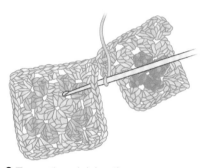

1 Work the first side of the current square including the first corner grouping (first set of 3htr or 3tr), then instead of making ch2 for the corner space, insert the hook into the corner space of the starting square from underneath as shown.

2 1dc into the corner space of the starting square (counts as first of 2-ch for the corner space), ch1, then work the second 3htr or 3tr grouping into the corner space of the current square as usual.

3 To continue joining the squares together, instead of ch1, work 1dc into the next side space of the starting square.

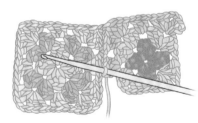

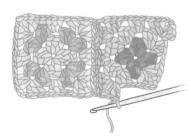

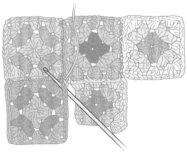

4 Work 3htr or 3tr in the next side space of the current square. Continue replacing each ch-1 at the sides of the current square with 1dc into the next side space of the starting square, and replacing the first of the ch-2 at the corner space of the current square with 1dc into the corner space of the starting square.

5 When the current square is joined to the starting square along one side, continue around and finish the final round of the current square as normal.

6 When joining a current square to two previous squares, replace both corner ch of the current square with 1dc into each adjoining square.

Sewing on buttons

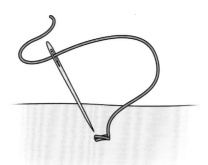

1 Mark the place where you want the button to go. Push the needle up from the back of the crocheted fabric and sew a few small stitches in this place.

2 Bring the needle up through one of the button's holes. Push the needle down through the second hole and the fabric. Bring it back up through the fabric and then the first hole. Repeat five or six times. Make sure you go up and down through the button's holes so the thread doesn't loop around the side of the button. If your button has four holes, use all four of them to make either a cross or parallel pattern. Finish with a few small stitches on the back of the crocheted fabric, and trim the thread.

Cross stitch

To work a cross stitch, work a diagonal stitch, then work back over it to complete the 'cross'.

Straight stitch

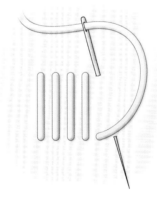

Bring the needle through to the surface of the fabric and then take it back down to create a small straight stitch. These can be worked as part of a design or facial features.

Tassels and fringes

Tassels are single clusters of knotted yarn ends; if they are repeated close together along an edge this creates a fringe. Use the same colour yarn as for your project, or choose a contrasting colour of your choice.

1 Cut strands of yarn to the length given in the pattern. Take one or more strands and fold in half. With the right side of the project facing, insert a crochet hook in one of the edge stitches from the wrong side. Catch the bunch of strands with the hook at the fold point.

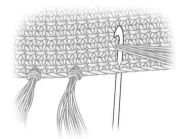

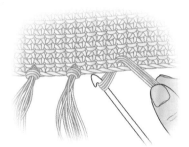

2 Draw all the loops through the stitch.

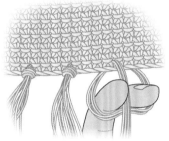

3 Pull through to make a big loop and, using your fingers, pull the tails of the bunch of strands through the loop.

4 Pull on the tails to tighten the loop firmly to secure the tassel.

Crochet stitch conversion chart

Crochet stitches are worked in the same way in both the UK and the USA, but the stitch names are not the same and identical names are used for different stitches. Below is a list of the UK terms used in this book, and the equivalent US terms.

UK TERM	US TERM
double crochet (dc)	single crochet (sc)
half treble (htr)	half double crochet (hdc)
treble (tr)	double crochet (dc)
double treble (dtr)	treble (tr)
tension	gauge
yarn round hook (yrh)	yarn over hook (yoh)

Abbreviations

approx.	approximately
BLO	back loop only
ch	chain
ch sp	chain space
cont	continu(e)ing
cm	centimetre(s)
dc	double crochet
dc2tog	double crochet 2 stitches together
dec	decrease
dtr	double treble
htr	half treble
htr2tog	half treble 2 stitches together
in	inch(es)
inc	increase
m	meter(s)
mth	month(s)
patt	pattern
rep	repeat
RS	right side
sp	space
sl st	slip stitch
st(s)	stitch(es)
tr	treble
tr2tog	treble crochet 2 stitches together
WS	wrong side
yd	yard(s)
*	repeat instructions from this point
[ ]	repeat instruction within brackets the number of times stated

Index

Suppliers

If you wish to substitute a different yarn for the one recommended in the pattern, try the Yarnsub website for suggestions: www.yarnsub.com.

UK

LoveCrafts
Online sales
www.lovecrafts.com

Wool Warehouse
Online sales
www.woolwarehouse.co.uk

Laughing Hens
Online sales
Tel: +44 (0) 1829 740903
www.laughinghens.com

John Lewis
Yarns and craft supplies
Telephone numbers of stores
on website
www.johnlewis.com

Hobbycraft
Yarns and craft supplies
www.hobbycraft.co.uk

USA

LoveCrafts
Online sales
www.lovecrafts.com

Knitting Fever Inc.
www.knittingfever.com

WEBS
www.yarn.com

Jo-Ann Fabric and Craft Stores
Yarns and craft supplies
www.joann.com

Michaels
Craft supplies
www.michaels.com

Australia

Black Sheep Wool 'n' Wares
Retail store and online
Tel: +61 (0)2 6779 1196
www.blacksheepwool.com.au

Sun Spun
Retail store (Canterbury, Victoria)
and online
Tel: +61 (0)3 9830 1609
www.sunspun.com.au

....

Acknowledgements

I would like to offer my thanks to the yarn companies that supported the projects for this book – Stylecraft Yarns, King Cole, James C Brett and We Are Knitters. Thank you to the fabulous team at CICO Books. Also, eternal gratitude to my husband, John, for always being my first supporter and embracing the everlasting yarn stash.